VOICES FROM THE EASTER RISING

VOICES FROM THE EASTER RISING

EDITED BY

Ruán O'Donnell
Mícheál Ó hAodha

MERRION
PRESS

Published in 2016 by
Merrion Press
8 Chapel Lane
Sallins
Co. Kildare

This collection © Merrion Press 2016

British Library Cataloguing in Publication Data
An entry can be found on request

978-1-78537-066-3 (Paper)
978-1-78537-067-0 (PDF)
978-1-78537-069-4 (Kindle)

Library of Congress Cataloging in Publication Data
An entry can be found on request

CONTENTS

PART TWO: OUTSIDE DUBLIN

PREFACE

The Easter Rising or 'Easter Week' is a phrase which resounds throughout the world today, whenever freedom from oppression in the history of small nations is discussed. While a great deal of attention has been paid in recent publications to the testimonies and recollections of the leaders of the Irish Volunteers and the most senior British statesmen who opposed their actions and attempted to counter them during that violent week, relatively little regard has been paid thus far to the testimonies of the protagonists on both sides who were not household names. The importance of these people in the shaping of modern Irish history cannot be underestimated.

Based on eyewitness accounts of the events of Easter Week, this volume provides a unique snapshot of how the Rising took shape and developed in Dublin, but more crucially still perhaps, in a range of other Irish cities, towns and villages. Here you will find the perspectives of civil servants and other members of the establishment working in Dublin Castle and within the British administration at this time, but also hitherto lesser-known accounts of Easter Week from within the IRB, the Citizen Army ranks and ordinary Irish people who were bystanders. These dramatic first-hand narratives, encapsulating men and women of a range of ages and perspectives – British, Irish, working class, middle class, urban and rural – afford an invaluable insight into this period and the aspirations and actions of the combatants. Powerful, painful and moving in equal measure, the testimonies collected in this volume bring to life once more voices that were frequently forgotten or neglected, voices that significantly expand our understanding of this momentous event in Irish history.

Dr Mícheál Ó hAodha
University of Limerick

The texts reproduced in this volume have preserved the original spelling of the writers and interviewees.

Leabharlanna Poibli Chathair Baile Átha Cliath

Dublin City Public Lib

DRAMATIS PERSONAE

Domhnall Ó Buachalla was a shopkeeper and Irish language enthusiast who expanded the Gaelic League in Celbridge, Kildare and befriended leading activist Patrick Pearse. He joined the Irish Volunteers and was the principal republican in the Maynooth sector. His militancy ensured that local Volunteers followed him into the G.P.O. on learning that fighting had erupted in the capital.

Captain Harry de Courcy-Wheeler of the King's Royal Rifles Corp, was Staff Officer to Major General William Lowe, commanding officer of the British army during the Rising. Based at the Curragh Camp in Kildare when news arrived that the Rising had begun in Dublin, he joined senior officers in Parkgate Barracks and, alongside Major General Lowe, took the surrender from the Rebel leaders on Moore Street, as well as the voluntary surrender of his first cousin's wife, Countess Markievicz.

Fr. Augustine and Fr. Aloysius belonged to the Capuchin Friary on Church Street, Dublin, a socially deprived part of the city which saw much fighting in the Rising due to its position within the heart of Ned Daly's 1st Battalion. Both men were trusted by local members of the Irish Volunteers and as the fighting drew towards a close endeavoured to ensure that lives were not wasted after the decision to surrender had been made. They ministered several of those facing British army firing squads in Kilmainham Prison.

The 'Lady Telegraphist' who recorded her impressions of the Rising was an employee of the G.P.O. when the rebels followed James Connolly's order to seize the building. She noted the reactions of the work force to brief detention and the loyal contribution of those who operated the Crown Alley Telephone Exchange in Temple Bar.

Elsie Henry lived in Ranelagh, an affluent south Dublin suburb, when rumours, news and evidence of political turmoil exploded. On friendly terms with many leading personalities, including Roger Casement, Eoin MacNeill and Bulmer Hobson, she followed the dramatic events unfolding around her with keen interest recorded in her diary.

Feargus 'Frank' De Búrca was one of the first and most prominent young republicans in St Enda's where he joined Na Fianna Eireann (NFE) and the Irish Volunteers. The son of a leading London-based Fenian, De Burca was privy to many of the illegal activities of Patrick Pearse and Con Colbert. He participated with the Rathfarnham Company, aka 'Pearse's Own', in the 1916 Rising.

Sir Alfred Bucknill was Britain's Deputy Judge Advocate General. Following a personal briefing by Prime Minister H.H. Asquith he travelled to Dublin to oversee legal aspects of quashing the Rising. Bucknill determined which legal protocols were used to prosecute the leading rebels and played a part in curbing the scope of courts martial planned by General Sir John Maxwell.

Desmond 'Des' Ryan was a former student of St Enda's College, Dublin, who following graduation took work in his Alma Mater where he functioned as an assistant to Patrick Pearse. A member of the Rathfarnham Irish Volunteers, Ryan was at Pearse's side in the G.P.O. and acted as his literary executor.

Dick Humphreys hailed from a comfortable and highly politicised family based in south Dublin during the Revolutionary period. A nephew of Michael 'The' O' Rahilly, de facto Quartermaster General of the Irish Volunteers, Humphreys gravitated into republican politics during his time as a student in St Enda's. He was one of the youngest participants in the Rising.

Áine Ceannt (aka Frances O'Brennan) married leading republican Eamonn Ceannt in 1907 after meeting in the Gaelic League and kindred cultural organisations. She interacted with many significant contemporaries in Cumann na mBan, of which she was a member, as well Irish Volunteers and Irish Republican Brotherhood. Ceannt was one of a number of Sinn Féin personnel who supported the militants. Her husband signed the 1916 Proclamation and was executed for being Commandant of the 4th Battalion in Dublin.

Louisa Hamilton Norway, wife of G.P.O. Manager Arthur Hamilton Norway, was privy to much of the inner workings of the British administration in Ireland and numbered Sir Matthew Nathan as an acquaintance. She exerted herself during Easter Week to maintain a telephone connection between Dublin and London.

Samuel Guthrie worked in the G.P.O. as Superintendent of Telegraphs. He was on duty in the capital when coordinated groups of specially equipped rebels cut numerous wires running under the streets of the inner city. He was among the first to warn the authorities that a Rising was underway.

Captain E. Gerrard, a graduate of Clongowes College, was commissioned into the Royal Field Artillery and served in the disastrous Dardenelles campaign in April 1915. Based in Athlone, Gerrard was off duty in Dublin when the Rising created confusion and inertia in the depleted city garrison.

Thomas Leahy worked in shipyards in England and Scotland before returning to Ireland where he was variously a member of the 2nd Battalion Irish Volunteers and the Irish Citizen Army. He experienced the Rising in some of the secondary outposts of the north inner city of Dublin which protected the approaches to the G.P.O. Headquarters of the Provisional Government. Leahy witnessed the evacuation of the G.P.O. and occupation of the Moore Street terrace where the decision to surrender was taken.

Maeve and Milo MacGarry belonged to a well-educated Dublin family of mixed political viewpoints. A suffragist and anti-monarchist, Maeve joined Cumann na mBan and Milo, a former student of St Enda's, the Irish Volunteers. Both siblings witnessed the drama and upheaval of Easter Week at close quarters.

Richard Balfe graduated from Na Fianna Eireann into the ranks of the IRB and Irish Volunteers. He participated in events surrounding the landing of weapons at Howth, County Dublin, in July 1914. Captain of 'D' Company, 1st Battalion, Balfe saw action in the Mendicity Institute and other sectors of the city centre during the Rising.

Annie O'Brien and Lily Curran, sisters born into the Cooney family in Dublin, were friendly with prominent revolutionaries in the capital, not least NFE organiser Con Colbert. Having joined Cumann na mBan they were active as auxiliaries in the 4th Battalion sector prior to and during the Rising.

John Joseph Scollan, a Derryman, led the Hibernian Rifles in Dublin during the Rising. The small but well organized militia were the armed expression of the Ancient Order of Hibernians (Irish American Alliance) which unlike their much larger rivals in the AOH (Board of Erin), enjoyed close links with the IRB in Ireland and Clan na Gael in the United States. Scollan was on good terms with socialist republican James Connolly with whom he had interacted during the protracted 1913 'Lockout' dispute.

Molly Reynolds hailed from a republican family and emulated her brothers who joined NFE by becoming a founder member of Cumann na mBan. This was encouraged by Bulmer Hobson, a close associate of her father, and in whose company she met Roger Casement and other leaders. Mobilised at St Stephen's Green, Reynolds was redirected to the G.P.O. by Margaret Skinnider where she assisted in the provision of medical care to wounded rebels.

Frank Gaskin joined the IRB in Liverpool in 1911 but by 1914 was living in Dublin as a member of 'D' Company, 4th Battalion Irish Volunteers. He participated in the Howth and Kilcoole gunrunning operations and was a member of the Dublin Centres Board chaired by Bulmer Hobson. During the Rising Gaskin took part in the raid on the Magazine Fort.

St John Greer Ervine, Belfast-born playwright and Fabian, was in Dublin on Easter Sunday 1916 as the first stirrings of the Rising reverberated. An acquaintance of W.B. Yeats, Ervine had links to the progressive Abbey Theatre and served during World War One with the Royal Dublin Fusiliers.

Michael Newell joined the IRB in Athenry, Galway, in 1908 and was engaged in land agitation in Connaught until obliged to relocate to Meath in 1911. Newell was an Intelligence Officer in the Dunboyne Irish Volunteers headed by Sean Boylan who interacted with Pearse.

Áine Ní Riain, a founder member of Cumann na mBan in Tullamore, Offaly, was visiting Dublin when the leadership of the Irish Volunteers was conflicted by news that the *Aud* arms ship had been intercepted. She witnessed the confusion occasioned when Chief of Staff Eoin MacNeill issued the 'countermanding' order requiring adherents to cancel the Easter manoeuvres planned as cover for a national uprising.

Daniel Tuite participated in Sinn Féin activities in Newry, County Down, before he joined the Irish Volunteers when they were raised in Dundalk, County Louth, in 1914. A follower of the Eoin MacNeill tendency after the 'split', Tuite took part in route marching, drilling and other paramilitary preparations in Louth and Meath.

Michael Gray was involved in the formation of the Irish Volunteers for the Maryborough area of County Laois towards the end of 1914. On Easter Sunday night, 23 April 1916, these Laois Volunteers demolished a section of the Abbeyleix-Portlaoise railway line. Their objective was to prevent likely British military reinforcements from reaching Dublin via Rosslare or Waterford once the Rising had begun.

Thomas Kelly joined the IRB in 1914 in Donoughmore, County Tyrone where his father was also a member. He travelled to Scotland for work where he met other Irish Volunteers and attended various meetings in Motherwell and the Sinn Féin Hall in Glasgow. Kelly returned to Ireland briefly for the funeral of O'Donovan Rossa in August 1915 and ultimately participated in the Rising.

Patrick 'the Hare' Callanan joined the Clarinbridge Circle of the IRB in April 1905 and was involved in land agitation which, in the sector, extended to cattle driving, breaking walls and shooting at the houses of landlords. In 1906 Callanan moved to Creggane, Craughwell, where the IRB's South Galway Circle, led by Thomas Kenny, was particularly active.

Michael Spillane and **Michael J. O'Sullivan** joined the Irish Volunteers in November 1913. In early 1914 Spillane became Centre of the local IRB which extended its influence into the larger organisation in Killarney, Kerry.

Riobárd Langford joined the Irish Volunteers in Cork from the Gaelic League which met at An Dún in Queen Street. The O'Growney Branch attracted Alice Barry, Annie Walsh, Tomás MacCurtain, Frank Daly, Martin Donovan and Seán O'Hegarty. Scholar Daniel Corkery and IRB man Terence MacSwiney moved in their circle, as did members of the AOH (Irish American Alliance). Langford was one of the first Section Commanders appointed in Cork City where he was 2nd Lieutenant of 'C' Company in 1914.

✳

Introduction

Following years of cultural and political revival, organised Nationalists who comprised the vast majority of Ireland's population in 1914 invested hope that the imminent devolution of Home Rule would provide a large measure of self-determination within the British Empire. Hostile anti-democratic forces, not least the paramilitary Ulster Volunteer Force, had spurred supporters of Home Rule to establish the countervailing Irish Volunteers (Oglaigh na hEireann) in Dublin in November 1913 under the nominal chairmanship of Eoin MacNeill. From the outset members of the illegal Irish Republican Brotherhood exerted much control in the organisation and prepared cadres for a more ambitious degree of political assertion. Backed by their strong North American affiliate Clan na Gael, the IRB intended to redirect the manpower of the much larger Irish Volunteers towards an insurrection that would achieve the sovereign republic.

A strategic opportunity arose on 4 August 1914 when Britain declared war on Germany. This promised to divert the bulk of the standing army to the battlefields of western Europe leaving Ireland relatively thinly garrisoned. The Royal Irish Constabulary and Dublin Metropolitan Police were unequal to the task of containing the Irish Volunteers whenever military support was unavailable. The protracted 'Lockout' trade union dispute of 1913–14 had disenchanted swathes of the urban population from the authorities. As the Volunteers spread throughout the country, supporters of the constitutionalist Irish Parliamentary Party joined en masse and by June 1914 were a major presence on its Executive. This presaged the September 1914 split in the movement when IPP leader John Redmond insisted that his followers should advance national interests as part of the war effort. The widening schism, paradoxically, enhanced the grip of the IRB core over the more militant elements that rejected Redmondite moderation. They had disproportionate access to modest quantities of weapons run into Howth and Kilcoole in July/August 1914, as well as the vital US connections which financed such activities.

CNG leaders John Devoy and Joe McGarrity encouraged IRB associates, namely Tom Clarke, Bulmer Hobson and Sean MacDiarmada, to prepare the ground for a revolution in Ireland. Recent acolytes Patrick Pearse, Joe Plunkett, Thomas MacDonagh and Eamonn Ceannt were among those tasked from January 1916 with devising contingencies. Socialist Republican James Connolly was co-opted to the discrete 'Military Council' bringing his well-trained Irish Citizen Army into the equation. The equally small but dedicated unarmed female auxiliary, Cumann na mBan, geared itself to provide logistic, communications and medical support. Other significant bodies included Na Fianna Eireann, the de facto youth wing of the IRB which provided in-depth and practical training to the new generation of republican leaders. The Hibernian Rifles, whose membership were drawn from the Ancient Order of Hibernian (Irish American Alliance), were well disposed and anxious to play their part. All rose in arms in Dublin on 24 April 1916 when the Provisional Government and Army of the Republic established headquarters in the General Post Office.

The pathway to proclaiming the Irish Republic at the GPO had not been easily navigated. Hopes that Germany would provide sizable quantities of war material were dashed at the last moment when the *Aud* arms ship was intercepted and obliged to scuttle off the Cork coast. IRB emissary Roger Casement was captured shortly after being landed by U-Boat on the rural Kerry shoreline and local republican commanders were arrested in consequence. MacNeill's belated realisation that a coterie attached to Clarke was manoeuvring assiduously towards revolution shocked him to the core. When it became clear that no irresistible military effort could be mounted in the immediate future he endeavoured to keep the Irish Volunteers demobilised so that they could fight another day.

Incompatible instructions reached all parts of the country creating chaos and inertia among the regional leadership. Most of those who turned out in Tyrone, Cork and Limerick returned home without firing a shot.

The main consequence of MacNeill's 'countermanding order' was that the 'six days of the republic' were concentrated in Dublin. Yet those who had hoped to hold out for two days in order to give meaningful effect to the declaration of Irish independence at the outset survived heavy British counterattack that left the city centre in ruins. Notwithstanding negative trends, numerous bodies of Irish Volunteers had stirred across the country and serious manifestations occurred in Wexford, Galway, Meath and elsewhere. Pearse, Commander-in-Chief of the Irish Republican Army, had difficulty arranging the surrender of the militants he had exhorted to rise. The execution of fifteen leading republicans in May 1916 proved, as expected, a catalyst in changing Irish public opinion from a desire for Home Rule to a demand for the Irish Republic. This volume provides first-hand accounts of the dramatic story from various political and geographical perspectives.

Dr Ruán O'Donnell
University of Limerick

PART ONE

INSIDE DUBLIN

✳

The Seizure of the G.P.O. Dublin by the Sinn Féin Volunteers on Easter Monday, 1916.

A Few Notes by One Who Was There

Looking back on the events that happened on Easter Monday, 1916, when the Sinn Féin Volunteers rose in armed rebellion and proclaimed an Irish Republic under the portico of the G.P.O., Dublin, the whole proceedings appear to have been more like a dream than reality. The dream is rudely dispelled, however, by paying a visit to Sackville Street, where the ruin and desolation caused by the gigantic fires that raged during Easter week is only too pronounced. The weather on Easter Monday was ideal for outdoor amusements, and the thought of one at least in the Instrument Room on that forenoon was that it was fortunate for the holiday makers that the sun shone so brightly. This train of thought, however, was roughly interrupted at 12 noon by the announcement from our Chief Technical Officer on duty that the majority of the lines running into the Instrument Room, including our cross-channel wires, had become stopped, due to the fact that the leading in cables in the basement had been cut. Almost simultaneous with the receipt of this information the news was brought that the Sinn Féin Volunteers had entered the public counter – the new office only recently opened to the public – had taken possession and had turned everybody else out into Sackville Street. Credence could not at first be given to this story, but the noise of breaking glass in the front of the building partly verified it, and on looking out over the top part of the window into Sackville Street it was only too evident that the story was true, as all the windows in the lower storey were being smashed from the inside, the broken glass being thickly strewn over the pavement. It was also seen that a number of the rebels guarded the entrance to the public counter with rifles and revolvers, whilst others were distributing to a crowd large poster sheets which proved to be copies of the Proclamation of the Irish Republic.

Since the beginning of the war we have had a military guard of a sergeant and half a dozen men to provide a sentry at each of the two entrances to the Instrument Room. About 12.30 p.m. the sergeant of the guard reported that the rebels were forcing the stairs leading up to the northern entrance. The corridor leading from the top of the Northern stairs to the Instrument Room – about 10 yards long – was then hastily filled with chairs, waste paper boxes and other portable articles that could be laid hold of in order to impede the entrance of the besiegers as long as possible in the hope that help would arrive in time to prevent them gaining possession. The sergeant and the guard could only stand inside the Instrument Room door ready to receive the attackers if they broke through the obstructions in the passage. The rebels then commenced to fire through the passage into the Instrument Room, and the noise thus made in a confined space greatly alarmed the female members of staff. When the corridor had been barricaded all the female staff were cleared down to the southern end of the room, and as matters became worse they were instructed to proceed to their Retiring Room on the southern landing and put on their outdoor apparel in case it became necessary that they should leave the building. About ten minutes to 1 o'clock a message was brought to the Superintendent from an officer of the Sinn Féiners who was stated to be on the southern landing to go out to him to make arrangements for the staff to leave the building. The Superintendent declined to go, sending word that he would not hold any parlay with the officer as he (the Superintendent) did not recognise the right of the officer to be where he was. (By this time all the females had left the Instrument Room.) A minute or two afterwards the officer in question, with a few supporters, came into the Instrument Room each being armed with a revolver and ordered everyone to clear out, at the same time ascertaining that no one was in possession of arms. This officer it was subsequently ascertained was The O'Rahilly.

By 1 o'clock the last of the male staff had left the G.P.O. building. The guards were made prisoners and detained. The officer and his party had gained access to the southern corridor through the dining-room by means of a flight of stairs leading from the Sorting Office to that room, and as there was only one sentry guarding the southern corridor he was easily overpowered. About 1.20 p.m. the Lancers arrived from Marlboro' Barracks and rode down the street from the Rotunda. About a dozen of them had passed the Nelson Pillar Monument towards Clery's shop when the fusillade was opened on them from the windows of the G.P.O. Several saddles were emptied and the horses stampeded, some of the later being badly wounded, two ultimately died, and their carcasses lay in the streets for some days. I was subsequently informed that four of the Lancers were killed and some wounded. The rest of the party retired down the side streets to shelter. When the firing had ceased several street urchins rushed out from where they had been sheltering in the adjoining houses, and helped to capture the riderless horses and led them away. One of these horses was badly wounded in the shoulder, and as it limped along a barefooted urchin managed to withdraw the trooper's carbine from its case and at once made all speed with it to the G.P.O. building and thrust it through one of the barricaded windows to a member of the *garrison*. It showed in a small way that the invaders of the G.P.O. had some sympathisers amongst the crowd outside.

All the windows of the G.P.O. in each storey were broken by the rebels and then barricaded with mail bags, tables, chairs and such like, in order that they could fire out at any relieving force that might make its appearance. A machine gun was subsequently erected by rebels on the roof of the G.P.O., and another on Clery's roof on opposite side of street. I think it was on Friday in Easter week that the G.P.O. was burned. The rebel garrison sought to make their escape through Moor Lane – opposite the Henry Street entrance to the G.P.O. – but were met by military machine guns and very few got away. The O'Rahilly was killed in this way. He was of gentlemanly appearance and good manner, and it must be said that he behaved most courteously in the matter of clearing out the staff in the Instrument Room.

It would appear that the rebels had prepared postage stamps for use under the *Republic*. They had seized a lot of British stamps in the public office and used them for sticking up on the walls near the G.P.O. the notices or proclamations of the Irish Republic.

Domhnall Ó Buachalla, Irish Volunteers, Maynooth, 1916.[1]

We received no orders or instructions prior to Easter Week. On Easter Monday afternoon I learned from a bread-van driver that fighting was taking place in Dublin between the Volunteers and the British military. I got on my cycle and proceeded to Dublin to get instructions and find out what we were to do. On approaching the Phoenix Park I heard firing, I think it was from the Magazine Fort in the Park. I proceeded down the northern quays. At the Mendicity Institute there were British soldiers taking cover under the Liffey wall on the north side of the river and avoiding the firing which was coming from the Institute. They did not stop me and I passed through. Further down the quays near the Four Courts, the Volunteers had a barricade across the street. I was halted here. I told the officer who was in command here who I was and where and for what I was going. He let me pass through.

I proceeded to No. 2 Dawson St. which I knew to be the Headquarters of the Volunteers, but found the place locked up. I started back for home and travelled via the N. C. Road. The British had a barricade on the street near Phibsboro Church. It was situated between Doyle's corner and the Church. I was allowed through here again without any interference. I cycled through the Park and back to Maynooth. On reaching Maynooth I found Tom Byrne of Boer War

---

[1] B.M.H., W.S. 194.

fame, and Tom Harris there. Byrne had come on from Prosperous. I do not know if he was sent down by Volunteer Headquarters to take charge in Kildare. The Maynooth Volunteers had mobilised in the yard of my house. There were about fourteen men present all told. They had the sporting guns and some rations. I got my rifle and we fell in on parade and marched to the College. Tom Byrne was in command.

Two R.I.C. men and a Sergeant had been observing us and when we marched out towards the College, they followed us. Vol. O'Kelly covered them with a revolver which he had and told them that if they came any further he would let them have the contents. They then went back to the barracks. We proceeded to the College and asked the President for his blessing. He said he did not approve of what we were doing. He gave us his blessing, however. When passing through the College the students were favourable to us and encouraged us. A servant boy in the College, who was not a Vol[unteer] joined us and came all the way to Dublin with us and fought there during the week. We came out of the College on to the canal bank and proceeded towards Dublin. For some portion of the way we travelled on the railway, and at other times through fields, until we arrived at Glasnevin Cemetery. We walked across the Tolka River which is about two feet deep and entered the cemetery. We had sandwiches to eat before leaving Maynooth and another on route. We got to Glasnevin about 2 or 3 a.m. on Easter Tuesday morning, and rested there. About 6 a. m. Byrne went into the city to see if the road was clear and he then came back and marched us into the General Post Office. There was a dead cavalry horse in O'Connell Street, otherwise everything was quiet. We got a cup of tea and some buns in the canteen from Desmond Fitzgerald. We were then sent to the Exchange Hotel in Parliament St.

We got into the Hotel by a back entrance and immediately were posted in positions at the windows. This was in the forenoon. We were not long there when a party of British soldiers arrived at the *Evening Mail* office, which is at the junction of Parliament St. and Dame St. One big soldier started to smash in the door with a sledge. I asked Byrne if we would fire. I do not know what he said. I put up my rifle and took aim at this soldier and fired. He dropped the sledge and fell forward and the man next to him fell also. The second man was behind the big soldier and, apparently, both of them were hit. Immediately the rest of our boys opened up with the sporting guns on them and in few seconds at least a dozen soldiers were lying on the Street. An amazing thing was that a priest appeared on the scene almost immediately and attended to the soldiers who were wounded or dead. We went on to the roof of the hotel to see if we could engage the soldiers in the Castle. The roof was heavily under fire from the Castle and the enemy had a party in the drapery establishment at the corner and junction of Dame St. and Parliament St. and opposite the *Evening Mail* office. This party were able to throw hand grenades at us and one of our garrison – a Dublin man – was badly wounded in the groin. Shortly after this we got orders from Byrne to go back to the G.P.O.

We left the hotel by the back entrance and proceeded back to the G.P.O. via the Metal Bridge over the Liffey. The garrison in the G.P.O. seemed to be well organised and everybody was going about their duties in an efficient manner. That evening (Tuesday) another man, whom I do not know, and I were detailed to proceed to the glass turret or dome of Arnott's in Henry St. This was to try and keep sniping by the enemy from Westmoreland St. under control. I was given good field glasses. We used bales of cloth to barricade the dome and try and make it bullet proof. There was sniping from the Westmoreland street direction but it was impossible to locate the snipers.

After some time I noticed that one of the upper windows of McBirney's drapery establishment on Aston Quay was opened, the rest being closed. I could see a waitress in her uniform carrying a tray past the window. It occurred to me that it was strange for a waitress to be on duty when the premises were closed being right in the centre of the area where fighting was taking place. I got my glasses on to the window and, as I suspected, I observed a soldier in a stooped position in the far side of the room and holding a rifle. I took aim at the window and fired. The first shot was high, hitting over the window. My second shot went thro' the top pane and my third also went into the room. I did not see the waitress any more after this. No firing took place from that window afterwards. That night I was called in from Arnott's and sent across to the Dublin Bread Company's premises in O'Connell St. which is now the Grand Central Picture House. It was occupied by the Volunteers. There was at this time a lot of sniping from Trinity College and I was sent there to try and deal with it. I engaged some soldiers on the roof of Trinity College and, while I drew back from the loophole in the barricaded window from which firing, a bullet came through and grazed my hair. I could see Liberty Hall from the window and observed the effect of the shelling by the British war vessel – the *Helga* – and saw some of the walls crumble and fall. That evening I was called back to the G.P.O. and placed at one of the windows. I noticed a Volunteer going around who did not seem normal. He had a shotgun with which he was continually 'fiddling'. He was near me and let off a shot which lodged in the books with which the window was barricaded. I jumped down and took the gun from him and threw it into a big wastepaper basket. I remained in the G. P. O. during the shelling of the place and until it took fire.

At this time the other side of O'Connell St. was on fire also and the heat was intense. The garrison of the G.P.O. under Sean McDermott fought the fire with hose and buckets, but it was no use and we had to get out. We had to move along Henry St. until we got opposite Moore Lane. We crossed Henry St. into Moore Lane and halted there and here the 'fumbler' with the gun was beside me again. He had the butt of the gun on the ground and a shot went off. The poor follow got the complete contents in his throat and died immediately. While we were there an officer asked for four men to do some job. I do not know what it was now. I can remember that three of us in single file were running down Henry St. towards Mary St. The enemy had a barricade across the street at Williams Shop. We were under fire all the time.

When halfway from Moore Lane to this barricade the man in front of me dropped, having been hit. Almost immediately, the man behind was hit also and I dropped down in the channel on the side of the street. I saw that a large window of Williams & Woods' shop was devoid of glass, apparently having come under the notice of the looters. I got up and jumped in through the window leaving my rifle on the path. When inside it struck me that there might be a shop hook and I searched around in the dark for it. I found one. With this I hooked in my rifle. There was a big number of young men inside, apparently after loot and making an awful amount of noise. I asked them to keep quiet, but it was of no avail, so I decided I was getting out of this. I took off my boots and, having discarded my rifle, tried to get out through back. The place was a mass of broken glass, jam, treacle, etc. I succeeded in getting out at the back and made my way along a lane towards Parnell St. After wandering around and eluding the British troops and barricades I eventually arrived at the Broadstone Station. In the meantime I had secured a pair of shoes. It was now Saturday morning when I arrived at the station. There was a guard of British soldiers on the gate and I was halted and placed under arrest. I was brought into the station and placed under guard in the ticket office. There were a few prisoners already there whom I did not know. We got no food or any refreshments. The following morning, Sunday, I was brought with the other prisoners to Richmond Barracks and placed in the Gymnasium. There was a big crowd of prisoners there at the time.

Captain Harry de Courcy-Wheeler, British Army, based at the Curragh Camp.

A t the outbreak of the Irish Rebellion on Easter Monday the 24th April 1916 I was stationed on the Curragh.

By Tuesday the 26th April 1916 all the available troops had left there by road or had been entrained at the Curragh siding for Kingsbridge, and were under the command of Brigadier General W.H.M. Lowe, C.B. who was appointed General Officer Commanding the troops engaged against the rebels in the Dublin Area.

On the 28th April General Sir John Maxwell, K.C.B., K.C.M.G., C.V.O., D.S.O. arrived in Ireland with plenary powers from the British Government, and was appointed General Officer Commanding- in- Chief the Forces in Ireland.

On the 28th April at 10.30 p.m. I received an order through the Garrison Adjutant to report immediately to General Lowe's staff at Headquarters Irish command Park gate street. I got my kit ready, borrowed a loaded revolver, overhauled my motor car and left the Curragh alone as the old water-tower clock was clanking midnight. The journey was uneventful, the roads being totally deserted until I was close to Island Bridge. The houses from there to Parkgate seem to have been occupied by the British Military as I was suddenly pulled up with the cry of 'Halt or I fire,' all along the line, and when the car stopped a rifle with fixed bayonet was thrust through the window, the password demanded and information as to my identity and destination. I said 'if you take that b----- bayonet away from my chest I will be able to give you the information you want.' I then showed the Sentry my instructions and he told me the way to reach Headquarters. From that point the whole City seemed to be in a blaze and rifle fire was going on in all directions and shells were bursting at intervals. However, there was no time to investigate, and I arrived at my destination at 1.45 a.m. The General and his staff had their Quarters in two adjoining rooms and were sleeping on the floor dressed in their uniforms. The telephone was going continuously and one of the staff officers asked me to take it over as they had had no rest for three nights.

All sorts of messages came through as to the disposition of troops, asking for orders, reports of snipers located in various and distant parts of the city, houses blown up and fires here, there, and everywhere, especially in Sackville Street and the neighbouring Streets. One message I recollect very distinctly, the Manager of a Bank in Upper Sackville Street telephoned that the Bank was on fire, that there was a Caretaker with a large family in the house and how were they to escape. Upper and Lower Sackville Street were being swept with rifle fire by snipers and the British Military were replying. I asked the General what was to be done about this family entrapped in the burning Bank, and he said 'tell them to march out with a white flag'. I 'phoned the Manager these instructions. Presently the telephone rang again from the Manager to say they had no white flag and 'would a Union Jack do?' That put the lid on it. So I advised him to be quick and to make a white flag or they would all be buried or shot! As I said, the telephone kept going continuously all night until 11.30 a.m. when I was relieved, and although I had taken charge of it, my brother Officers got little rest. In the morning, one of the General's Orderlies brought us a cup of tea and bread and butter but a very limited supply, as rations were very uncertain and few and far between. We had to go to Kingsbridge Station to get something to eat end to Ross's Hotel near the bridge.

At 12.30 infomation arrived that a Red Cross Nurse was waiting at the Parnell Monument who had been sent by Commandant Pearse to negotiate terms of surrender. The General ordered me to accompany him. It was a difficult matter at that time to reach Parnell Monument from Headquarters Irish Command in Parkgate Street, and it necessitated a zigzag course in and out of side streets and taking the intervening corners at high speed owing to the sharp-shooters who were posted at vantage points on the roofs of the houses; two bullets did get the panel of the near door of the car, which was an Official saloon car supplied for the use of the Staff, but owing to the skilful driver and the speed, I expect the snipers did not realise who was in it until it had skidded round the next corner.

Eventually the General and myself arrived at a small Newsagent's shop a few doors from the corner of Great Britain Street, where it joins Upper Sackville Street at the Parnell Mamment, and I was afterwards informed that this shop belonged to Mr Tom Clarke, one of the seven Signatories to the Republican Proclamation. The General communicated the terms to the Sinn Fein Nurse, and she was allowed half-an-hour to return with the reply from Commandant General Pearse, who was in command at the rare of the G.P.O. and controlled Moore Street and the adjoining thoroughfares. Upper Sackville Street was still swept by snipers, and while waiting for the return of the Sinn Fein Nurse, General Lowe who was in his Staff Uniform, and a very conspicuous mark, strolled into Sackville Street to note the position. The whole of Upper and Lower Sackville Street was held by the Rebels at this time, and I felt responsible for the General's safety, and pointed out that he would draw the fire on himself if spotted. He made little of it, but in the end I persuaded him to return to the Newsagent's shop, and wait there for the despatches from the Rebel Commander-in-chief. Soon after the Sinn Fein Nurse returned with a reply imposing conditions. These were refused, and the General sent her again to say that only unconditional surrender would be accepted, and that she could have half-an-hour to return with the reply.

At 2.30 p.m. Commandant General Pearse, Commander-in-Chief, surrendered to General Lowe accompanied by myself and his A.D.C. at the Junction of Moore Street and Great Britain Street, and handed over his arms and military equipment. His sword and automatic repeating pistol in holster with pouch of ammunition and his canteen which contained two large onions were handed to me by Commandant General Pearse. His sword was retained by the General. The other articles are reproduced in the photograph. There were two Army Official Motor cars waiting. Commandant General Pearse accompanied by the General's A.D.C. was driven in the General's Car, preceded by the General and myself in the other car to Headquarters Irish Command to interview General Sir John Maxwell, the British Commander-in-Chief. After the interview Commandant Pearse signed several typed copies of his manifesto, which was dated by himself, Dublin, 29th April, 1916, and reads as follows:

> In order to prevent the further slaughter of Dublin citizens, and in the hope of saving the lives of our followers now surrounded and hopelessly out-numbered, the members of the Provisional Governments present at Headquarters, have agreed to an unconditional surrender, and the commandants of the various districts in the city and country will order their Commands to lay down arms.

After signing these documents Commandant General Pearse was conducted to a sitting-room at Headquarters, I was ordered to keep guard over him, and was locked in the room alone with Commandant Pearse. I was handed a loaded revolver with orders to keep it pointed at Commandant Pearse, and to shoot should he make an effort to escape. This was a very responsible and serious order to obey and to carry out should it have become necessary, but Pearse did not seem in the least perturbed and greatly to my relief I was on this duty for only fifteen minutes when I was sent for by General Lowe and another Officer was sent to relieve me. He ordered me to go at once to the Castle, show the manifesto of Commandant General Pearse, the Commander-in-Chief, to Commandant Connolly in command of the Irish Citizen Army who had been brought in wounded and a prisoner, and get him to sign the document or a similar Order to his own men. When I arrived at the Castle, part of which had been turned into a Red Cross Hospital, I was brought up to the ward where Commandant Connolly had been carried. He was in bed, and I waited beside him while his wounds were being dressed, I told him my orders and asked him did he feel well enough to comply. He said he was, and he read the manifesto which was signed by his Commander-in-Chief. Comnandant Connolly then dictated the following, as he was unable to write himself, which I wrote down underneath

Commandant Pearse's typed manifesto and it was signed, and dated April 29/16 by Commandant Connolly:

> I agree to these conditions for the men only under my own Command in the Moore Street District, and for the men in Stephen's Green Command.

This document containing the orders of Commandant Pearse and Commandant Connolly was presented on the following day by me to Commandant Thomas MacDonagh who added the following words and signed and dated it 30.IV.1916 3.15.p.m.:

> After consultation with Commandant Ceannt I have confirmed this Order agreeing to unconditional surrender.

I shall deal with this later on.

Previous to the surrender of Commandant Pearse I was with the General, at the top of Moore Street which was barricaded with sandbags, behind which the British were firing and were being fired at by the rebel forces. There was the body of an Irish soldier lying in Moore Street and I was informed that it was The O'Rahilly who had been shot shortly before.

The document referred to above in my own handwriting ordering the surrender of their Commands by P.H.Pearse, Commander-in-Chief, Janes Connolly, Commandant General Dublin Division, and Thomas MacDonagh, Commandant, has been reproduced in facsimile in several publications.

On the night of the 29th April, General Lowe accompanied by myself and two other members of his staff paraded at the Parnell Monument to receive the surrender of the rebels in accordance with their Commander's instructions which had been communicated to their respective Commands in the meantime, and up to 10.30 p.m about 450 surrendered there. Of these I took down the names and addresses of 84 and delegated other Officers to take the remainder. The prisoners were drawn up in line and I walked down the ranks taking down each name and address as given to me. As it was physically impossible for me to write down all the names I sent word to the General that I required assistance and he then detailed fourteen other Officers to help me. The lists made by these Officers were handed in to the Assistant Inspector General of the Royal Irish Constabulary at a later date.

I received many expressions of kindliness and thanks from my rebel countrymen with whom I came in contact and to whom I was opposed. Some of those whose names and addresses I took down personally on that night have held, and now hold, the highest positions in the Service of the State, they fought to found, and others have passed away. I have reproduced in facsimile the pages of my note book on which I wrote down by their own direction those names and addresses. They were then marched into the enclosure in front of the Rotunda Hospital.

That night I received orders from the General to be at the Bank at the corner of Rutland Square and Upper Sackville Street at 8 p.m. the following morning, Sunday, 30th April, 1916, to meet the Sinn Fein Nurse, as she was then known to us, and afterwards as Nurse Elizabeth O'Farrell, who had undertaken to conduct me to the Headquarters of the various commands in and around the city for the purpose of communicating the orders to surrender detailed above. A military motor car was in waiting, driven by one of the Royal Army Service Corps motor drivers, with the Sergeant Major of the 5th Royal Irish Regiment as escort. I was unarmed, but Nurse O'Farrell carried on old white apron on a stick as a flag of trace, and she and I sat behind.

I decided to go to the College of Surgeons, Stephen's Green, first, which was strongly held by the rebels and which was keeping up a continuous fusilade with the British garrison in the United Service Club and the Shelbourne Hotel. On the way I had by the General's instructions ordered an escort of military to be in readiness at Trinity College to take over the College of Surgeons if the rebels surrendered. At Lambert Brien's Shop in Grafton Street my motor was brought to a standstill owing to the cross firing, and I decided to allow the Nurse to proceed alone and deliver the document at the College under cover of the white flag, as both she and it would be recognised and respected. She returned about 9.30 having delivered the message. Thence I endeavoured to drive her to Boland's Bakery,

Ringsend, but owing to the barricades across Lower Mount Street, and having tried all the routes down by the river which were held by the rebels, and reports of continuous firing further on, I had again to allow the Nurse to proceed on foot to deliver the document under cover of the white flag. When she returned unsuccessful at about 11.30 I took her up again and drove her through the Castle up Ship Street to St Patrick's Park, being the nearest point that the motor could approach to Jacob's Factory as this and the surrounding neighbourhood was very strongly held by the rebels. I was to meet her again at 13 noon. It will be noted that these visits were for the purpose of handing in the orders to surrender to the various Commandants, not to receive their surrenders. Nurse O'Farrell was very intimated with the situation of all these Commandes, and had no difficulty in directing the motor which was the best route to take and where to go next, so that no time was lost on that account. While waiting in St Patrick's Park for the Nurse to return I went to the Castle and obtained informtion from the Garrison Adjutant that a telephone message had been received from the O.C. Troops, Shelbourne Hotel that the Republican Flag over the College of Surgeons had been hauled down, and that troops were required to take over the College and the surrender of the Garrison.

I motored back at once to Trinity College and ordered the Military Escort which was in waiting to proceed up Grafton Street as far as possible, and to keep the men out of view of Stephen's Green as there was still sniping from various points. From there I went to the Kildare Street Entrance of the Shelbourne Hotel and interviewed the O.C. troops who pointed out the position from the top window where he had his maxim gun placed. Having informed him of my plans, and having telephoned to the O.C. Troops United Service Club not to 'open fire' as I was about to receive the surrender of the rebels, I returned to Grafton Street, picked up the Sergeant Major with the motor and drove to the front door of the College of Surgeons. I ordered the Sergeant Major to bang at the door, and having waited for a reasonable time without any response, a civilian signalled that there was some excitement going on down York Street. I went there and saw that a white flag was hanging out of the side door of the College. Two of the rebel leaders came out, advanced and saluted.

The Commandant stated that he was Michael Mallin and that his companion was Countess Markievicz, and that he and his followers wished to surrender. The Countess was dressed in the uniform of an Irish Volunteer, green breeches, putties, tunic and slouch hat with feathers and Sam Browne belt, with arris and ammunition. I asked her would she wish to be driven in my motor under escort to the Castle, knowing the excitement her appearance would create when marching through the streets. She said 'No, I shall march at the head of my men as I am second in Command and shall share their fate.' Accordingly I requested her to disarm, which she did, and when handing over her arms she kissed her small revolver reverently. In addition to this small automatic pistol, Countess Markievicz was armed with a German Mauser pistol, which she also handed to me. This latter was retained by General Lowe until leaving the Curragh, when he presented it to me, and both are reproduced in the photograph in this article. Commandant Mallin was not armed and I requested him to order his followers to lay down their arms in the College and march out and form up in front of the College. While they were doing so, I sent a message to the escort in Grafton Street to come up, as there were no British troops picketing this part of the city and I had only 25 men in Grafton Street. I then inspected the rebels in the College and ascertained that they had disarmed, and inspected the arms in a large room in the upper part of the building, portion of which had been curtained off as a Red Cross Hospital. Commandant Mallin and the Countess Markievicz accompanied me during my inspection. The whole building was in an indescribable state of confusion and destruction, furniture, books, etc., being piled up as barricades and the large picture of the late Queen Victoria torn to pieces and destroyed. Food, clothes, arms, ammunition, mineral waters, surgical dressings were mixed up and lying about in all directions. On my enquiring about the wounded, the Countess informed me that they had been removed. There was one prisoner, Mr Lawrence Kettle, who was handed over to me, and whom I drove to the Castle and handed over to the authorities there. Having carried out the inspection, I ordered the Commandant to march out his followers, whom he informed me numbered 109 men, 10 women, the Countess Markievicz and himself. I 'phoned from the nearest telephone instrument – the Mineral Water Direct Supply Co. at Stephen's Green – to Headquarters to inform the General of this surrender.

Immense crowds of civilians had in the meantime assembled in York Street and Stephen's Green, as there were no troops guarding this portion of the city, and it was with much difficulty that the Officer commanding the escort which was small succeeded in getting the rebels away in safety. Tremendous cheers greeted the rebels as they surrendered, and the crowds followed them and continued down Grafton Street until I succeeded in getting a cordon across the street which held the crowds back at the point of the bayonet and allowed the escort and their prisoners through to safety to the Castle. In the meantime I had detailed one N.C.O. and four men to take charge of the College until a stronger guard could be obtained. The escort and prisoners reached the Castle Yard in safety at 1.45 p.m.

I then proceeded to my rendezvous with Nurse O'Farrell at St Patrick's Park but was informed that she had not returned from Jacob's Factory although it was 2 o'clock. She was to conduct me to the South Dublin Union, Marrowbone Lane, Distillery and the Broadstone district. In the meantime General Lowe had accepted the offer of two Franciscan Monks to persuade the Rebels to surrender, and at 3 o'clock the General arrived with his staff. Commandant MacDonagh and the two monks arrived with a white flag. By order of the General I then drove to the back of Jacob's Factory, accompanied by his A.D.C. Commandant MacDonagh and the two monks, and waited outside in the street, one of the monks holding up the white flag continuously. We were detained there for a considerable time, sniping going on close by but not into the street. Finally the rebels agreed to surrender St Patrick's Park. Thence the same party drove to the South Dublin union where there was also a considerable delay in obtaining an interview with the Commandant who also finally agreed to march his men to St Patrick's Park. From there accompanied as before I drove to Marrowbone Lane Distillery over which floated the Green Flag. Dense crowds surrounded the motor car and we were warned that irrespective of the white flag and the monk who was carrying it, anyone wearing khaki would be fired upon. In spite of this nothing unpleasant happened. However, although there seemed to be great relief in this district that hostilities had ceased it was perfectly plain that all the admiration was for those who had surrendered.

After this I drove back again to Jacob's Factory. Here there was a long delay owing to Father Augustine having gone into No. 15 Peter's Street at the rere of the Factory with MacDonagh, and I was informed that he was receiving final instructions from the rebels before they surrendered. Eventually, owing to the dense crowds and delay as I had to go from there to Boland's Bakery at Ringsend with Nurse O'Farrell to deliver Pearse's Notice at the Headquarters there, I ordered the motor to go to Ship Street close to St Patrick's Park and wait there for the surrender.

An unpleasant incident then occurred. Commandant MacDonagh shortly afterwards arrived followed by crowds and accompanied by the Monk with a white flag, and stated that although his men had laid down their arms in order to surrender, the soldiers had opened fire on them, were throwing bombs into the house, and that the military had broken into the Factory and were killing his men, and that he had seen one of our soldiers taking up a position in the factory and was using his bayonet. I told MacDonagh that it was impossible, as there were no troops there, and that if it was one individual soldier I did not understand why he and his men could not deal with him. He replied that if they interfered with the soldier they were afraid it might be serious for then. Commandant MacDonagh was so positive about the occurrence that I reported it to the G.O.C. 176th Inf. Brigade and brought MacDonagh before him. The General stated that there were none of his troops there, and he instructed me to ascertain at the Castle whether any troops had been sent independently. Accompanied by General Lowe's A.D.C. I went with MacDonagh to the Castle and brought him before the Colonel in Command, who also stated that there were no troops at Jacob's. I then drove MacDonagh back and he requested some Officers to go and ascertain the fact, took upon myself to advise strongly against this and refused to allow General Lowe's A.D.C. to go, pointing out to the G.O.C. 176th Inf. Brigade and to the O.C. Troops in the Castle that it was an impossible story got up for some purpose. Accordingly, I told MacDonagh to return accompanied by

Nurse O'Farrell, a priest and the monk who was most vigorous in denouncing the proceeding, and to order his men to surrender, the G.O.C., and 176th Inf. Brigade and the O.C. Troops in the Castle having pointed out that if there were soldiers firing at the rere of the Factory it would not prevent his own men from coming out at the front of the Factory! Shortly afterwards the two Monks, the Priest and Nurse Elizabeth O'Farrell returned and stated there had been no foundation for the accusation against the military, that none of the Commanders had been injured, and that it was looters who had broken into Jacob's and were doing mischief. I immediately reported this to the G.O.C. 176th Brigade and to the O.C. Troops at the Castle, and asked them to hear the priest on the subject, which they did. Shortly afterwards the Commander from Marrowbone Lane and from the south Dublin Union arrived and laid down their arms in St Patrick's Park along with the commander from Jacob's. I then set off again with Nurse Elizabeth O'Farrell to drive her to Boland's Factory at Ringsend, but as it was now getting dark and she said she would prefer to go in the morning. I drove to Trinity College with her and telephoned to General Lowe for instructions. He replied that the following morning would do, and that in any case it was reported that the Ringsend commands had surrendered to the O.C. Troops, Ballsbridge, and to place Nurse Elizabeth O'Farrell in the Red Cross Hospital at the Castle until the following morning leaving her in care of the Matron and not as a prisoner.

It was on account of this previous surrender that I did not come in contact with Commandant de Valera who was in command at Boland's Hill, but I have since met him annually under the most friendly conditions.

On the night of the 30th April I was invited by Capt. Purcell to accompany him in his high dog cart to visit the scenes of the fires which were raging especially in Upper and Lower Sackville Streets and the adjoining thoroughfares. This was the first time, owing to the surrender of the Rebels, and the cessation of hostilities that it was possible for the Fire Brigade to get down to work and try to combat the fires.

Rev. Father R. Augustine, O.F.M., GAP., formerly of The Priory Church Street, Dublin.[2]

In the late hours of Saturday evening I suspected there was something unusual on foot, and on Easter Sunday morning I received an unsigned letter – handed in at the door – telling me not to hold any communication that might come from Eoin MacNeill. On Monday we were at dinner, between 12 and 12.35 o'clock, when a Brother who had been at the Convent door, rushed into the Refectory saying that a boy had been shot in Church Street and that the Volunteers were out.

About an hour later two or three of them were at our Bowe Street gate, two in the passage between Bowe Street and Church Street, commonly called the Chapel Yard, and barricades were being erected with great haste in Church Street. One of these was opposite our Church, another at the first turnings below the Church on the right, and another at the top of the Street where Church Street intersects North Brunswick Street. Heavy firing was heard at intervals and this, as I observed while standing at the front door of the Church, seemed to have the effect of intensifying the zeal of the boys in strengthening the barricades.

[2] B.M.H., W.S. 920

I moved about freely for the next few days doing whatever I could in a spiritual way for the boys who had taken over the Father Mathew Hall as a first-aid post whence serious cases were removed to the Richmond Hospital. The side hall at the left, as you enter from the Street, was devoted to the wounded, and on Wednesday a few soldiers were confined in the main hall facing the entrance. The members of the Cumann na mBan were most devoted to those, who had been wounded in the fight. On Tuesday and Wednesday morning as I was near the Church a fine young Volunteer approached me. He told me he had been married that morning, but would like to go to confession before taking up his post. He left his gun standing against the wall, made his confession in the nearest confessional, and outside I bade him good-bye and gave him a blessing as he went off in the direction of North King Street. On Wednesday I had a chat with Piaras Béaslaí who thought all was going well. On Thursday, after 3 pm. as far as my memory serves me, after having attended to some calls in the district, I felt a strange urge to go and see how things were going in the Four Courts. I went off alone down Church Street and having succeeded in getting in was hailed by the boys with great delight. Some asked for confession and I began work at once. One of those who came was Patrick O'Connor who belonged to the 4th Battalion of which he was a Section Leader and who is now in the National Library, Kildare Street, where we met again in 1941 or 1942 when I was collecting matter for my book – *Footprints of Father Theobald Mathew, O.F.M., Cap., Apostle of Temperance*, and revived many memories. Another was Frank Fahy, the present Ceann Comhairle. After confession I remember well telling him of some foolish talk that I had heard to the effect that the garrison would soon retire and fight their way into the open country. He looked at me, smiled and said that was impossible as they were being gradually surrounded. While I was still hearing confessions Liam O'Carroll came and told me that one of the Volunteers was badly wounded. I hastened away with him, descended to the yard where Liam told me to bend as low as I could as the cemented path along which we ran under the windows was covered by a sniper until we came to an open door at the opposite side, 'Now, Father', said Liam, 'be careful in crossing here.' 'Better for us to go singly', said I, 'as we'll give the sniper less chance that way. Now Liam, you first.' He cleared it at a bound. 'Good man,' said I, clearing the passage as quickly as I could, and bursting into laughter as I felt I had cheated the sniper.

We mounted a stairs together and he showed me into a room where the poor wounded Volunteer lay with a Sacred Heart badge in his hand. The window was not too well barricaded with books and, while crossing for something, he was shot through the left lung. He now lay on his back on the floor, his head held up by a brave Cumann na mBan girl. I had to tell her bend lower as I was afraid she might be seen by the sniper. The few in the room knelt and I, lying on my side on the floor, anointed the brave man of twenty-nine summers who a day or two later died a grand catholic death in the Richmond Hospital kissing his crucifix and murmuring ejaculatory prayers. Many and many a time since then have I thought of that afternoon during which I felt the urge to go to the Four Courts. I understood the urge better and thanked the good God that during all those eventful days I bore about with me the Holy Oils... Having heard some more confessions I left about six o'clock and having reached the barricade where Bowe Lane intersects Church Street I stopped to have a few words with the young Volunteer who lay crouched beneath it. 'You're in danger, Father', he at once said to me, and I remember well answering: 'I know I am, but I want to get home.' Realising that there were snipers about I did not wish to go along the Lane as I would be exposed too long to their vision, and decided quickly to take the shorter way to the Church Street gate leading to the Convent.

I had scarcely left the barricade and come into view when a bullet hissed through the air. I flopped at once, got up quickly, and ran to the near gate protected by the houses, entering the Church immediately to say a prayer of thanks to the Lord for my escape. I wish here to state quite sincerely and candidly that during the whole week as I moved about I had no fear, but others may find it interesting to know my real feeling. Well, I felt that I might be badly wounded, but that I would not be killed outright.

On Friday activity in the city became more intense and machine gun fire was heard more frequently. More wounded were brought to the Father Mathew Hall and the English snipers were busy. Some shots from the direction of Smithfield pierced some of our windows and shattered a stairs at the Smithfield end of our top corridor. That large window I had flung up on the previous Wednesday when I looked out and down Bowe Street to see if the enclosed bridge that spans the street and joins the two portions of Jameson's Distillery had been blown away. The Volunteers, suspecting that the English might enter from the Smithfield side and cross over to the other and rain down bullets on the Volunteers that were in the Chapel yard, decided to blow up the connecting bridge. But the experience was not a success. When the bullets came through the window out of which I had looked for a few minutes only two days previously, I thanked the good God for His loving mercy in my regard. But my heart was sad in the evening when I heard that a dear pupil of mine at Rochestown College, whose laugh I loved, had perished while doing something similar to what I had done. Dominic O'Donoghue, a boy of about seventeen years of age, had been playing with a companion under the eyes of his Father in an open space at the North Dublin Union. When both gave up they agreed to mount the clock tower to have a look round at the fires, as I was told later, that now blazed in the city. Dominic put his head through the first window or aperture he found... and his companion, mounting higher, did the same. A sniper at the Broadstone saw them and sent them into eternity. Father Albert, who had been active between the Union and the Hospital since the previous Tuesday, was quickly on the spot and anointed both of them. The English were gradually closing in on us and two of the Fathers remained in the Father Mathew Hall this (Friday) night to attend to the wounded and be on the spot for further possible eventualities.

On Saturday morning, the 29th, things had become more serious, and British soldiers had succeeded in taking possession of some houses on both sides of North King Street. After early Mass and a hasty breakfast I relieved the two Fathers in the Father Mathew Hall and remained there the whole day. There was a couple of bad cases and we had no Doctor up to the present. About three o'clock in the afternoon, when the military were already firing on the barricade at the Hall, I sent Micheál Ó Fóghludha, under a white flag, to secure one if at all possible. As he did not return, after about an hour or so

I suspected something untoward had happened, and sent a young fellow named Doyle, with a white flag and a Red Cross one, to see the Colonel in charge to give him a letter I had written. In this I explained that I was a Capuchin priest, that the Hall was being used as a hospital, that I was there in charge of the wounded, and that, under the circumstances, I asked the favour of an interview. Having seen the Colonel at the barricade, after some considerable delay, he brought back to me the oral answer he had received and delivered it to me in words that I shall never forget. He said; 'Father, we were all rebels and outlaws and that we would get none of the amenities of war.'

I remember well smiling at the words because many thoughts arose in my heart, but after thinking a while I took counsel with some of the wounded who now began to suspect that surely we would be shelled. I saw clearly that this might possibly happen and decided therefore, to go to see the Colonel myself. But before doing so, as the following day was Sunday and as I did not know what might become of it, I was anxious to tell the other Fathers what I was about to do, so that in the event of my not returning the Masses would be arranged by the Vicar. The Fathers were just finishing supper as I entered the Refectory about 6.20 p.m. and after I had told them briefly what had transpired during the afternoon and what I was now about to do to prevent slaughter, Father Aloysius, who was then Provincial, at once volunteered to accompany me. With a warm 'God-speed' from the rest of the community we returned to the Hall and, accompanied by Doyle, who bore a white flag, we proceeded to the barricade at North King Street and asked to see the Colonel. Between two soldiers with fixed bayonets we were led up to a certain point in the street, and while we waited there, we saw three companies of soldiers marching down towards the barrier we had left, and also an armoured car and an ambulance quite near. Colonel Taylor came at length and having heard what we had to say, spoke some words. I knew the situation at first hand hence Father Aloysius thought it proper that I should be spokesman. I then told the Colonel what I had already written him, that we were using the Father Mathew Hall as a hospital, that there were several serious cases there, and that we asked for a truce not only to look after our wounded properly, but also – I felt I was playing my trump card – to hand over two English soldiers who were detained there as prisoners. To our astonishment he replied not a word, but turning abruptly to the officers near him, he consulted for a short time, and then left the shop without having spoken a word to us.

We remained there for some time, and when the Colonel did not reappear, we again asked to speak to him. A few officers, one of them General Lowe's son, walked down the street with us and we again met the Colonel near the corner where Church Street intersects North Icing Street. In a moment or two, as we were speaking to the Colonel, Micheál Ó Foghludha rushed across and, addressing me, complained of the way we had been treated. Just then some shots fired by the Volunteers struck the pavement, and the Colonel, angrily seizing Micheál, shoved him roughly to the other side of the street, covered him with his revolver and told him tell his to stop the fire and that if they fired again he would be shot. He did this in a hoarse voice still holding his white flag. and then I turned quickly to the Colonel and said: 'Will you, Colonel, grant the truce and promise me, on your word of honour, that if the Volunteers don't fire, your men won't fire.' He replied: 'I promise and I grant the truce until 10 o'clock on to-morrow morning.' Not knowing then who was in command I moved a little up the street and spoke to the Volunteers many of whom by this time had their heads out the windows.. 'Boys', I said, 'I want to speak to you', and a loud shout came in reply: 'Go on, Father.' I then told them that we had obtained a truce until the morning and that the Colonel had promised they would not fire if the Volunteers promised not to fire. 'Will you promise?' Another shout came 'We will, Father.' The Colonel was quite satisfied and we parted. We loitered about for a while chatting to the Volunteers and then went down to the Father Mathew Hall to give all there the news. Arrangements were made for the transfer of the cases to the Richmond Hospital and those who wished, nurses and patients, were told they could go home.

I wish to state here most definitely and solemnly that at this time I never thought of, much less uttered, the word 'surrender', nor did I know anything of the document in which Pearse said that he and his fellows of the Provisional Government had agreed to unconditional surrender and, ordered the Commandants of the different districts to order their men to lay down arms. I knew nothing of the surrender of the General Post Office which had taken place before 4 o'clock, nor even of the surrender of the Four Courts that took place an hour or two later. The first intimation I got of this was on the following morning under the following circumstances. About 6.30 on this Sunday morning, the 30th., I went up Church Street and spoke with some of the Cumann na mBan girls who were still in the Hall and some of the Volunteers who were standing at the windows of the houses. I said a few cheery words to them and told them that I was returning now and would offer up Mass for all of them. I was partly rushed and waiting for the clock to strike before going out to say Mass at 7 a.m. Father Columbus, who had been away since the previous Thursday, opened the sacristy door and told me of the surrenders and of Pearse's document. Even then I doubted and asked him if he had a copy. 'No, Father', he replied, 'but I saw it and had it in my hand.' 'But', I rejoined, 'I'm sure our men won't surrender unless they see a copy. Could you get one?' 'Of course I can', he answered, starting off at once to the Four Courts, where he was not so successful as he had anticipated.

As he was not back at 8 o'clock I, being anxious, spoke to Father Alcysius and we decided to walk over to the Castle where we soon met Brigadier General Lowe who received us in a very gentlemanly manner. I told him we had heard of the two surrenders, that a truce had been granted in our area, but that we were in quest of Pearse's document as we felt the Volunteers in our area would never lay down arms until they felt quite sure about it. He assured us the document was genuine, that typed copies had been made of it, but that, unfortunately, he could not lay his hands on one just now. 'But', he added, 'Connolly is here and would reassure you on the matter, if you were to see him.' 'Of course', we replied, and he at once led us to where the leader of the Citizen Army lay in bed. General Lowe remained outside. We entered, passing the armed sentry at the end of the room near the door, and I remember well, just as if it were but yesterday, the feeling of admiration in my heart as I laid eyes for the first time on this man of fine head and noble brow. Approaching his bedside I asked him if the document said to have been signed by

Pearse was genuine, and he assured me in the affirmative. 'Did you also sign it?' I then asked, and he replied at once 'Yes'.

Then, as I turned to leave him, he said 'But only for the men under my own command'. These words are indelibly imprinted on my memory, and I am all the more anxious to record them here because I have seen another account in which it is stated that it was General Lowe put him the question. The General was a gentleman; he recognised the delicacy of the situation; he knew our anxiety about the document; he trusted us fully and did not enter the room.

The General then, being still anxious as we were to get at least a copy of the document so that it could be shown to the Volunteers who had not yet surrendered, placed his car and chauffeur at our disposal and we drove at once to Arbour Hill Detention Barracks to see Pearse who, after a short while, was ushered into the room by a soldier who then stood at the end with loaded rifle. Pearse advanced with noble mien and such soldierly bearing that the word 'Napoleonic' shot at once through my brain. In answer to my question he said that he had signed a document of unconditional surrender stating the reasons why he had done so, but that one of our Fathers had been here a short time previously, and as he assured him no copy of it could be found, he wrote another of which the following is an exact copy: 'In order to prevent further slaughter of the civil population and in the hope of saving the lives of our followers the members of the Provisional Government present at Headquarters have decided on an unconditional surrender, and Commandants or Officers commanding districts will order their Commands to 'lay down arms'.

A Lady Telegraphist.

I went on duty at 8 a.m. Easter Monday. At about 12.20 p.m. I was relieved for luncheon. I went into the dining-room and shortly afterwards one of our girls came in saying the Volunteers had taken the Sorting Office. Several other clerks then came in looking very frightened, and told us that the Volunteers were proceeding up to the Instrument Room. By this time we were all beginning to realise that matters were serious, and just as I was going back to the Instrument Room one of the male clerks entered the dining-room and said something to the waitress, whereupon they all ran towards the door.

I then made enquiries and was told that the Volunteers were coming up the stairs, and that the best thing to do was to remain at the end of the Instrument Room. I went to the Instrument Room and found that all the clerks had left their circuits and were mostly in groups looking for the most part very pale. I looked out of the windows onto Sackville Street and saw crowds of people looking up at the G.P.O.

We were all anxious at this time to get out of the office, but we were told that no one could leave the building as the entrances were barricaded. The report of a revolver at the Henry Street end of the Instrument Room was next heard, and the Superintendent ordered all ladies into the retiring-room. We hurried in and put on our outdoor garments so as to be in readiness to leave, although we did not know what might happen next. The room was rather congested but everyone was cool and there was no unnecessary excitement. We stayed in this room for about a quarter of an hour when we were told that ladies could leave the building. We were conducted by one of the Volunteers through the dining-room into the yard, and after some little delay in opening the gate we passed out feeling greatly relieved, but fully aware that we were still in danger from stray shots. One of our lady Supervisors bravely refused to leave the building. The sergeant of the guard having been wounded in the head our lady Supervisor rendered First Aid, but as the wound was rather serious she was permitted to bring him to Jervis Street Hospital and have it dressed. She returned with the sergeant and remained in the G.P.O. until about 5 p.m.

(N.B.- This permission was only given on their word of honour to return which they bravely fulfilled although the Jervis Street authorities tried to persuade the sergeant to stay.)

The Dublin Telephone Exchange is, as stated earlier in this article, situated at Crown Alley, near Dame Street, and the devotion of the Telephonists to their duty during a most trying week has been referred to in the local press as worthy of special comment. It was to be expected that the courteous and able District Manager and his male staff would stick to their posts, but one would not have wondered if the nerves of the ladies had proved unequal to the strain. Such, however, was not the case even when the operators were at intervals told to lie on the floor during the rattle of rifles and machine guns. They wept but carried on the work notwithstanding the fact that the switchboard and ceiling were scarred with bullets.

For the first two days groups of operators relieved each other impelled to make the perilous journeys to and from their homes by a sense of duty, but by Wednesday morning conditions had become so bad that they had to settle down in the Exchange for the rest of the week. Expeditions for food were made at great risk by the male staff, and beds and bedding for about forty persons were secured.

The military defence of the Exchange had been undertaken by a body of the Royal Irish Rifles, and barricades had been constructed of stationary presses, pads of tickets and sand from the fire buckets.

More than once members of the Engineering Staff risked their lives in repairing lines wilfully damaged by the rebels.

Rev. Fr. Aloysius, O.F.M. Cap., Capuchin Friary, Church St., Dublin. Chaplain to Irish Volunteer Leaders, 1916.[3]

It was my office as Priest that brought me into touch with the happenings of the period. I shall follow notes which at the time I jotted down as an aide-memoire and which later appeared in the Capuchin Annual – indeed I can give you little more – just the notes expanded here and there. Circumstances created so many contacts between Church Street and the participants in the Easter Week Rising that people were led to think that we were in the secret and were aware of the preparations. But that is not so. The truth is that it all came on us as a surprise, as it did on most people. On Sunday night the Opening Concert of the Father Mathew Feis was held in the Father Mathew Hall. The House was full and I remember well how Miss Joan Burke sang the 'Minstrel Boy' with a spirit that electrified the large audience – the atmosphere seemed charged and I rarely saw a gathering so enthusiastic. Of course there had been rumours of all sorts in the City that day. There had been preparations for a Parade of Volunteers and it had been called off and that was enough to account for the tense spirit and the pitch of enthusiasm that

[3] B.M.H., W.S. 200

characterised the meeting. Perhaps some of those present were in the know – perhaps some of the artistes had an inkling or suspicion of something. I do not know.

Next morning – Easter Monday – I walked over to Gloucester Street to say Mass at the Convent. On my way I noticed some Fianna scouts on bicycles – and later passing to Gloucester Street I met Pádraig Pearse and another Volunteer on bicycles. They rode by without recognising me – they were evidently intent on reaching their objective in time. Pádraig Pearse wore a loose overcoat or mackintosh which covered some baggage. They had come into Gloucester Street from Rutland Street, I understand and the volunteer who accompanied Pádraig, I was later informed was Willie Pearse. I at once concluded that there was something in the air – probably they had decided to attempt the parade in spite of the authorities. On my way back to Church Street I passed several individual volunteers – some on bicycles. Shortly after 12 o'clock as we were at luncheon we were startled by rifle fire; and very soon word was brought to the Friary that a little boy had been shot near the Father Mathew Hall, and a wounded man was also brought to the Friary, and a number of terrified children crying came to us for shelter. By 1.30 p.m. barricades had been erected in Church Street and were manned by Volunteers. The Father Mathew Feis was in session and the children were hastily got under the stage for safety until it was judged wise to send them home. An Australian who happened to be in Dublin passing through Church Street stopped to speak to me – I was standing at the Church Gate. He told me that he was a doctor and he offered his services to render any assistance needed. He attended to the wounded man who had been brought to the Friary.

Towards night, volleys of firing became more frequent – and at midnight it became so violent that it seemed to be at our very gates. The volunteers rang the house bell to tell us that the military were actually in Bow Street. They were mistaken however. What had happened was that an attack was made by volunteers on the Quays on a military detachment with ammunition. On Tuesday morning volleys of rifle fire were frequent. A request was made by the Richmond Hospital for the services of some of the Fathers as wounded men were arriving there. A few of the Fathers went and took up residence at the Hospital for the remainder... first aid, and Cumann na mBan girls attended to emergency cases. Some of our Fathers were also constantly in attendance, Serious cases were removed to the Richmond. Rumours had been current the previous day that the G.P.O. and Castle had been taken by the Volunteers and that the Magazine (Powder) in the Park had been blown up...

News had reached us of the death of Sean Connolly who had been shot at the City Hall or Castle. The Volunteers took possession of the newly built (but unfinished) Corporation Houses in Church Street. The windows were protected with sandbags. Next day (Wednesday) the wildest rumours were in circulation but no incident of special interest was reported. The rifle firing and machine gun firing was continued through the day. On Thursday vary extensive fires could be seen and as far as we could locate them they were principally in O'Connell Street, and G.P.O. and Clery's seemed to be involved. The rifle and machine gun volleys were almost continuous. The Volunteers had taken prisoners – soldiers from Linenhall Barracks and a D.M.P. man, and had them working at filling sandbags in the Father Mathew Hall. On Friday the machine gun firing was continuous and there were many explosions from bombs or hand grenades.

We heard the heavy boom of cannon from the direction of the Bay. This was Friday and owing to difficulties of transport food as running short and it was difficult to obtain milk. The Volunteers worked very hard to bring up provisions. And I should here recall the fearless conduct of the young Fianna who braved all danger and kept communications going between various posts and rendered valuable assistance in maintaining supplies. A sad occurrence was reported today from the North Dublin Union. Two young fellows climbed to the top of the clock tower only to be caught by snipers from Broadstone and fatally wounded. The firing was very intense all through Friday sight and without cessation until 3 to 4 p.m. on Saturday afternoon. Many explosions, and many buildings could be seen blazing. The number of wounded was increasing and many cases were brought to the Father Mathew Hall. By 4 p.m. the Military were as far as the junction of King Street and Church Street and were firing on the Church Street barricades The Cumann na mBan girls at the Father Mathew Hall were very excited and naturally feared for the poor wounded under their care. A message had been sent under a white flag to acquaint the military that the Hall was being used as a hospital but it had no effect. Father Augustine despatched Micheál O'Foghludha with a white flag to secure a doctor but he was detained by the military. A second messenger bearing a white flag and Red Cross flag and a note to the Commander was sent. In the note Father Augustine informed the Commander that he was a priest and asked for the favour of an interview at the barrier as the Hall was used as a hospital and had several very serious cases. The reply was oral: The military would grant none of the amenities of war but would treat them as outlaws and rebels. The position was desperate and Father Augustine and myself decided that there was no option but to go ourselves and seek an interview with the Officer in command. Accompanied by Volunteer Doyle who carried a white flag we passed the barrier and between two soldiers with fixed bayonets we went to North King Street until we reached opposite the new houses near Lurgan Street where we were told we should wait the arrival of Colonel Taylor who was in charge.

While we waited there three large companies of soldiers marched by and an armoured car and an ambulance stood near. The Colonel then arrived and listened to our statement: he made no answer but unceremoniously turned and walked off. A long time elapsed – to us it seemed an hour, so anxious were we for the safety of the poor patients in the Father Mathew Hall. Then we saw Col. Taylor at the corner of Church Street, and we approached him. He very cooly informed us that a truce had been arranged. While with the Colonel Micheál O'Foghludha came to complain, that the soldiers had prevented him from going for a doctor. Just as he was speaking some shots rang out from a house between N. King St. and N. Brunswick Street; and turning to Foley Col. Taylor brutally shouted, at him to stop the firing or he would shoot him, and ordering him to the other side of the street he kept him covered by his revolver. Poor Foley, exhausted and hoarse, tried to tell the Volunteers that there was a truce and asked them to cease firing. Father Augustine stepped forward and appealed to them, too, and informed them that Col.

Taylor had told us that following advice to surrender from Pearse a truce had been made. The Volunteers believed it was only a ruse of the Military and would not believe it. However they agreed to keep the truce for the night on our undertaking to see Pearse in the morning at the earliest moment and satisfy ourselves and them of the genuineness of Pearse's message We than returned to Father Mathew Hall and gave word to those in charge of the wounded. Arrangements were at once made to transfer the wounded to Richmond Hospital.

And now we come to the second chapter of the tragic story – the Sunday of the Surrenders. Father Augustine and myself celebrated Mass about 7 o[clock] and after a cup of coffee and a very light meal of bread only we walked to the Castle to seek a permit to see Pearse. We had an interview with Brigadier General Lowe who was in command of the British Military Forces. He received us very courteously and promptly granted us the permit to see Pearse, at Arbour Hill. The General suggested that we should see Connolly also as he was responsible for the Citizen Army, and he took us to the room in the Castle where Connolly was a patient. In our presence he asked Connolly if his signature to the letter advising surrender was genuine. Connolly's reply was: 'Yes, to prevent needless slaughter.' He added that he spoke only for his own men. General Lowe then placed his car at our disposal, but he appealed to us to proceed to Jacob's Factory after we had seen Pearse and assured the Church Street Volunteers of the genuineness of the message. He told us that the Volunteers in Jacob's were still holding out and that he had not succeeded in getting the message to them. It would, he said, be a great charity if we could do this as otherwise he would be obliged to attack and demolish the Factory with great loss of life. We drove to Arbour Hill, saw Pearse, and were assured by him that he had signed the letter.

Elsie Henry
Ranelagh

25 April 1916

No post by the mail and vague and alarming rumours of a Sinn Fein rising in Dublin. We got the mail train, 5.20 p.m. and met Mr Forbes in it. He knew very little, but said the Post Office and Stephen's Green is in the hands of the Sinn Feiners, and that they have shot the station master at Westland Row. The train ran in to Harcourt Street instead of Westland Row, and Peter met us at Ranelagh with a car. It is quite true, and everyone was unprepared. General Friend is in London, and there is only enough military to keep it 'localized'. The Sinn Feiners have the GPO and are barricaded inside. All wires have been cut and we are without communications to England or the rest of the country. They have the line from Kingstown to Westland Row, and they have Kingsbridge station, Jacob's factory, Guinness Brewery, and the quays, and the Four Courts. Annie went all over town yesterday and saw a flag flying from the top of the GPO, the republican colours, red, white and green, and on it the words 'German and American Allies Help'. A machine gun is mounted on the top of the Post Office and they were firing with it.

Wednesday 26 April 1916

The firing continues; they have the gas plant and the power station of the Tramway company, so no trams are running. It is a glorious warm spring day, the trees all bursting into bright green and the birds singing. It is perfectly quiet here, but cyclists bring along all sorts of rumours. Peter and Peggy have gone to the College.

At 1.30 Peggy and I went down, as the Depot should have opened. We went by Fitzwilliam Place and Baggot Street. Everywhere deserted and dead with a few people stealing about, or talking in knots, and children playing in the street. The police are confined to barracks, but this morning Peggy saw twelve of them taking shelter under an arch, while some small children played in the road with occasional bullets flying over them...

At 4.30 I started for the St. John staff meeting in Dawson Street, and remembering Dr Mather Thomson [sic] was Staff Surgeon, went to his home. We walked down together, a fearful uproar of big guns and maxims going on continuously at Ringsend, they said at Boland's bread factory which the Sinn Feiners occupy. The firing was incessant. At the corner of Merrion Square and Clare Street a rifle cracked somewhere close to us. All shops are barricaded and closed. Some windows were broken in Nassau Street and the City is terrible, and Nobletts sweet-shop has been ransacked.

The office in Dawson Street was closed, so we came back. In Baggot Street we could see fighting at the Bag. St. [Baggot Street] Bridge end. Dr Thomson thought he saw a man fall, and went on ahead to see could he help. It was a sniper who had been caught red-handed. Two soldiers had crawled along the roof from one house to another and dropped on to the window from which he was firing. We came up Fitzwilliam Place, and on Leeson Street Bridge I met Dr and Mr Webb. She had telephoned to the Vice-Regal Lodge for orders for the V.A.D.s, and got the reply we were to do nothing and above all not to wear uniform. Sir Matthew [Nathan] is at the V.R. [Vice-Regal] Lodge and we suppose Dorothy is with him. She was to go to Foxrock on Monday, but she cannot have got away.

I went to Mabel Dickinson to tell her that much and she said troops had been arriving all day from England, and passing at the end of Marlborough Road. General Friend has returned on a gun-boat, and Lord French is said to be with him. The fighting has raged round Beggar's Bush Barracks, the Veteran Corps is shut up in there, Charlie Dickinson, Prof. Wilson, and Mr R.A. Anderson among them. They have plenty of food, and are only short of tobacco and razors! The Veteran Corps had been for a long route march on Monday, simply because it was Bank Holiday, and were struggling home along Northumberland Road, when suddenly they were fired at from windows, and four killed instantly, and some wounded. They went into Beggar's Bush Barracks, which had been their headquarters, and are surrounded by Sinn Feiners, or at any rate totally imprisoned there.

A young man came in, belonging to the motor garage at the top of Dawson St. His chief is away, and the next in command dying from wounds in hospital and he is in charge. He cannot do very much except go and look at the place, and yesterday got a bullet through his hat cycling there. He was in Stephen's Green itself today, there were dead men just inside the gates, he said the 'trenches' were pathetic, just little scooped-out hollows and bits of bushes stuck in front, no cover at all. Countess Markievicz, in men's uniform, with a cigarette in her mouth and a pistol in either hand was holding up the traffic. She shot a policeman dead.

Thursday 27 April 1916

This morning there was a great rush for provisions. By 12 o'clock many shops in Ranelagh had been cleared out and were closed. Neither loaves nor butter to be had. The baker cannot reach us as he is the other side of town. It is extraordinary to see the shops emptying. Annie and I carried home oatmeal and some provisions: flour can hardly be had. This afternoon I went over to St Mary's; they are moving house. The vans were there and the men quietly shifting furniture. The streets are quite empty except for people walking with provisions in their arms, and a few cyclists eagerly surrounded by pedestrians. General Friend has issued a proclamation ordering everyone to be in his house from 7.30 p.m. – 5.30 a.m., and not to approach the firing area, as the military won't be responsible.

From St Mary's I went on to the Wrights. Mrs Fleming, one of our Depot workers, has been shot and is in a nursing home. There is still no word of AE [George Russell].

Firing began at 4.30 this morning and has gone on intermittently all day. Peter saw a house in Harcourt Street on fire this morning, opposite the 'Winter Garden' pub. People strolled about but nobody did anything. Columns of smoke rose last night from the City, but impossible to locate it. After supper I went in to the Beattys. Joe Beatty was back on sick-leave from his regiment, but he has been called out again to act as guide. The British troops have been arriving on foot from Kingstown with no one to guide them geographically as to Dublin and they have been walking into death traps, particularly Carrisbrook house, facing Ballsbridge. Joe saw Mr Sheehy Skeffington and two men shot in Portobello barracks yard this morning. He did not know the other two.

There is a repeated report that a German boat has been caught off the Kerry coast with Sir Roger Casement and German officers on board. But we are utterly cut off from all communications, and all sorts of wild rumours and stories are in circulation.

A mail boat got in about 11 o'clock today, and the passengers walked from Kingstown. Mr Beatty knew one man on it who got into Dublin this evening. He had a *Sketch* with him, and Mr Beatty says Birrell is making jokes about the situation.

At 7 p.m. the gun-fire began in earnest. It has moved further citywards. We heard they were fighting in Brunswick Street this afternoon, so they must have got Westland Row and be pushing towards the G.P.O. The city is very dark for there is no gas, and tonight there are no lamps lit at all in this quarter.

10.30 p.m. There has been a great flare of fire or smoke ever since 7.30, impossible to locate but in the Westland Row or Sackville Street direction. The machine guns have never ceased since 7. The night is absolutely calm and still and the clocks strike the hours. The fire is awful, and the rattling guns.

The wretched men knew nothing of what was coming on Monday: only a minority of them knew. Most of them thought it was a Bank Holiday parade and many tried to get home after they realised, but could not. Connolly (Larkin's man) is in command of the G.P.O. and Westland Row, it is said, and McDonogh [sic] of the Northumberland Road end, and Countess Marckieviecks [sic] in Stephen's Green. But that is only hearsay.

11.45. The firing is getting worse.

Friday 28 April 1916

At 12.30 midnight the firing slackened, but began again about 2.a.m. fairly continuously. The firing continued all day. Dr Winter came 11 a.m. and reported Miss Reed had returned from London and was in 'Ivanhoe', with the Sinn Feiners in her gate-lodge. He cannot get to Steevens [Hospital] as it is impossible to cross the city. Mrs Pollok came at 11.30, Uncle Ned at 12. He tried to get to Plunkett House, but a sentry of whom he was trying to enquire the way, pointed a bayonet at him. AE has returned, last night, and had to walk from Clare, with an occasional car. It took him three days. Bea came at 2 and we walked together down Wellington Road to Landsdowne Road. Everything is quiet there, a lovely clear cloudless day. The fighting has been appalling – Evelyn and Con were shattered by it. Evelyn saw a woman throwing stones at a baker's boy this morning because he had no bread to give her. The shops are shut except for a few that have side doors, and there are queues of people waiting outside these.

The Wrights came at 4.30. [Peter brought flour]. Last night going home, they came on about twenty-five soldiers creeping along under the shadow of a wall at Oakley Road, close to MacDonagh's house, Sunnyside. They had their fingers on the triggers and motioned away the Wrights who hurried on. As they came to Rathmines church, a man ran out of a door, looked up and down the street and started to run, then thought better of it and dropped to a rapid walk till he got round a bend, then he just flew.

At 6 the Coles came. They had been in to Bray for provisions. The stock had given out and the grocers had met and decided to send a ship to Liverpool for more. Mabel [Dickinson] came in at 6. She has no further news about the Veterans at Beggar's Bush.

Another mail [boat] has come in from England, but no civilians are allowed on board.

Military have been pouring in from Kingstown in one unbroken line, horses and artillery. About 4.15 three private motors packed with military tore past up to Clonskeagh, and two hours later heavy covered wagons containing men, came in from the Clonskeagh district; a motor ambulance followed.

8.30 p.m. The sky is still red with the same fire; it is said that the whole block between O'Connell Bridge and Abbey Street is destroyed.

The firing goes on but nothing like so violent as last night.

Mabel found four or five soldiers sitting in a bunch in Marlborough Road, and seeing them very hot and tired, asked the officer mightn't she bring a bucket of water and give them drinks. He replied very curtly 'No'. She said it was a pity, and he replied 'Those are the orders, and there is every necessity for them.'

Some of the soldiers thought they were in France, as they had been bundled off without any word, and had had a railway journey and a sea journey, and concluded they had reached France.

Every day feels like a whole week.

Saturday 29 April 1916

Firing went on all night, with occasional big booms. At 11 a.m. I went down to see Dr Ella Webb; she is working at the temporary hospital at 40 Merrion Square. They would be glad of sphagnum dressings. I fetched Mrs Wright and Bea in a car, and we took a clothes basket. Connor put us down at the corner of Baggot Street and we walked to the College. As we went in, two repeated collapses of brick buildings rattled down somewhere near by. College looked barred and bolted. Empty. We left the basket and reported to Dr Webb. She said the hospital was filling. So at Leeson Street Bridge we found an ancient growler [horse-drawn cab] and drove out to Anglesea Road. By infinite luck the Registrar [of the College of Science] was on his doorstep. We got the master key and returned by Ballsbridge and Baggot Street. The Horse-Show grounds are full of military and horses. At Boland's [sic] bread factory opposite a long queue of people were waiting to try and get bread. Military are on Baggot Street Bridge. We got down again to the College and collected the sphagnum pads and some lint and gauze lor Nettie, who has wounded in her home. We carried the things along Baggot Street and down Fitzwilliam Street into Merrion Square. The City of

Dublin Red X people have a temporary hospital, at no. 40 further down. The fighting is all along Lower Mount Street. One man said 'It's a hot place you girls', but once into Merrion Square it was utterly deserted, just like 4 o'clock on a bright summer's morning. The birds all singing. There are sand-bags barricades all along the lower side of Merrion Square and the military firing from behind them. Soldiers were lying flat on the pavement, and taking cover behind lamp-posts. The firing was continuous and horrible. The column of smoke is still rising darkly from the Sackville Street direction.

Dr Lumsden and other devoted men in white coats and red crosses were there and Miss Blandford doing secretarial work. A priest and a clergyman were standing in the hall. Miss MacDonnell has taken night duty as matron there. The packing room is turned into an extempore theatre with operating tables. There are about twenty cases upstairs. One boy is shot through the lungs and dying. A woman leading a child was coming out crying as I went in. It is awful. A rumour came through that the Sinn Feiners had surrendered, but was immediately contradicted by telephone.

We reported to Dr Winter and Miss Winter gave us tea. We carried the dressings to Nettie and then tried to get home. Leeson Street Bridge was closed, so we went round Hatch Street to try Charlemont Bridge, meeting the Bests, also homeward bound. Mrs Best says it is true that Sir Roger Casement was taken from a collapsible boat landing in Kerry on Wetlnesday and taken to the Tower and shot. We reached Charlemont Bridge, and the military were packed into the houses and on the roofs of the houses on opposite sides. The houses on the city side were crowded with people, and 'Halt' rang from all quarters. We 'halted' up against the advertisement hoardings, in the middle of nothingness. We should have got through, only that someone lost his head and became hysterical, and shouted and made such a fuss that he drew attention from all sides, and we quite expected he would draw fire. We retreated, they, the Bests, to the Lysters, and we to Dr Webbs, where we failed to get on to anyone by telephone. So, making one last effort to get home, we came up Leeson Street and marched on to the bridge. 'Halt!', and we threw up our hands at a sentry pointing a bayonet at us. 'We have finished work and are going home, may we pass!', 'Ow, Oi carn't let yer owver' [sic], said the distressed sentry, The sergeant came up with a reassuring smile 'Pass!' and we 'passed' through a barricade of boxes, cases, old grates and all sorts. But for our uniform we shouldn't have got over.

Rumours keep rushing along that the city Sinn Feiners have given in, that the military are encircling the town, and are going to hem them in, and search the streets. There is nothing confirmed. Further rumours say a truce has been called to parley. No firing at all occurred from 5 till 7.30, then it began again intermittently. At 6.30 I got home to find kind Professor Cole had been in to say Augustine was in Ringstown, safe and well, and would get a military pass, and would arrive at 5.p.m. or, knowing we were all well, might cling to the baggage and stay the night in Kingstown. There are no Irish papers, but stray copies of the *Daily Mail* and *Sketch* brought over on the mail were selling for 1/- each. We have not had English or European news for five days, but the fictions have been stranger than truth could ever have been.

Mrs Rice, who works at the Depot lost her husband in today's fighting. The great difficulty is to bury the dead. They buried some today at St. Bartholemew's church (Elgin Road), where no one has been buried before, but it is a terrible difficulty, and also identifying the dead Sinn Feiners, who have no identification discs, and nobody knows what they are doing with their dead, or how they are getting their wounded attended to.

Sunday 30 April 1916

The firing went on till 2 p.m., probably all night. Some seemed to be in Rathmines and big guns sounded from the direction of Ringsend. Another lovely cloudless day, and fruit blossoms in full bloom.

At 1.30 Augustine arrived and said he had left London on Friday evening.

Feargus (Frank) De Búrca, Member of 'E' Company, Fourth Battalion, Dublin Brigade (Rathfarnham).[4]

Easter Monday

I was aroused from a sound sleep by Bulfin and told to get up immediately, that we were mobilised for Rathfarnham Church at 10 a.m. I was soon up and dressed and joined my companions in the refectory where we sat down to a good substantial breakfast, the last we were to enjoy for some time. After breakfast we donned our equipment and made our way in two's and three's to Rathfarnham Church. Mrs and Miss Pearse met us at the entrance gate of the 'Hermitage' and bade a fond farewell to each. I found it very hard to move quickly as I was carrying extra equipment for a Volunteer I was to meet at the Church. It was funny to meet the usual Bank Holiday hikers on their way to the mountains oblivious of the stirring events that were about to take place.

When we arrived at the Church we met other members of 'E' Company from the district but we had to wait a considerable time for some who lived a distance from the Church and who had received the order to mobilise later than we had. However, we mustered 57

---

4 B.M.H., W.S. 694

strong when we got the order to march. Just before we set out Eoin MacNeill approached our leaders and warned them that we were being led into a trap; that we should disband immediately and go home. He was told that we were acting under orders from our own Commandant. However, on getting the order to march we set off at a brisk pace to the tram terminus. We boarded a '17' tram, one of those open-top vehicles which are not to be seen now-a-days and the driver got orders 'full steam ahead to O'Connell Street'. Our destination was Liberty Hall.

The first sign that there was anything unusual in the air was at Jacob's Biscuit Factory. When passing there we noticed a large crowd of civilians men and women being ordered back by Volunteers with fixed bayonets. Jacob's factory was in the hands of the insurgents! The excitement was commencing. On down George's Street our tram rattled its way. Near the junction of George's and Dame Streets we heard a burst of rifle fire, the attack evidently on Dublin Castle. Our tram stopped right opposite the Bank of Ireland. Evidently the situation had become too hot and dangerous for our driver. He just left the tram there. We got out, formed four-deep and marched via College Street, Tara Street and across Butt Bridge into Liberty Hall. We were assigned positions immediately. Along with others I was ordered to take up a position on the roof. On my way across to the parapet overlooking the Liffey, my foot went down through slates, plaster and all. I had great difficulty in extricating myself. I thought at the time that this building wouldn't stand very long against enemy bombardment and I was glad when, after about ten minutes, we were ordered to proceed 'at the double' to Headquarters in the G.P.O. I remember C. McGinley was in front of me. We 'doubled' up Abbey Street and across O'Connell Street into Prince's Street. O'Connell Street was thronged with sightseers, some dumbfounded at the sight while others raised a cheer. The G.P.O. had been charged promptly at mid-day by the Kimmage Company and all inside had been ordered to clear out. All was bustle and excitement when we arrived in Prince's Street. As we were entering Prince's Street there were shouts, 'Here come the Lancers!', from some of the onlookers. We were immediately given the orders, 'About turn', 'Fix bayonets', etc. 'Twas a false alarm however as far as our group were concerned.

The Lancers had charged up from the Parnell Monument but, on running into a blast of fire from the G.P.O., they turned around and retreated.

The problem facing us now was how to get into the G.P.O. as the main entrance was locked for the moment. There was nothing we could do but clamber in one by one through the side window near the corner. Two of our Company stood at the window and helped each man as he came along to climb up on the window-ledge. 'Twas at this time that Volunteer Jack Keeley got mortally wounded. I was quite close to him when he fell back into a comrade's arms. He was our first casualty. It has never been ascertained whether the shot that killed him came from the enemy or from one of our own men. When I got through the window I found myself in a small room, the door of which was locked but, as the partition wall did not extend to the ceiling, I succeeded in climbing over it. In the meantime Lieutenant Boland had managed to burst the lock by firing into it a reckless thing to do, no doubt. Eventually we all got inside and out to the main yard at the back.

Shortly after our arrival the tri-colour was hoisted on the flagstaff at the left-hand corner facing Prince's Street. Commandant Pearse read aloud to the public on the street the Proclamation the Irish Republic and copies of the Proclamation were posted on the walls and pillars of the building. When Lieutenant Boland had reported our arrival to Commandant Pearse, we were ordered to take up a position on the roof, to which the access on the Prince's Street side, was by a spiral staircase at the back. Brian Joyce and I were stationed beneath the tri-colour at the Prince's Street corner. We were soon joined by an old friend, Eoghan Ó Briain, one of the few who was always present at our social gatherings in St Enda's. We were delighted to have him with us he was so good-humoured. The rest of the Company occupied a position over the porch of the G.P.O. and the corner opposite the Pillar. As most of the barricading and window-smashing had been done when we arrived, our main duty was to keep a watch out for the enemy as he was expected to attack any hour. We had a supply of the home-made bombs in front of us and we got detailed instructions how to use them if the soldiers succeeded in getting near the entrances. As no attempt was made to rush our position during the week, we were saved the trouble and risk of using these 'bombs'. One of our officers, Lieutenant Liam Clarke, received severe facial wounds when he was unloading some bombs from a handcart prior to distribution to the men. He had to be removed to hospital and was unable to participate in the fighting.

As far as actual fighting was concerned, there was nothing doing in our department on the first day. From all around us we could hear bursts of rifle and machinegun fire as the British troops were taking up attacking positions: Our forces held Jacob's factory, the Mendicity, the Four Courts, Boland's Mill and certain houses between these outposts. Rumours of all kinds were floating around 'The Volunteers were rising throughout the country.' 'All Kerry in a blaze.' 'German submarines were operating in Dublin Bay.' Heartening news for us certainly. I was elated but soon disappointed when Jimmy McElligott joined us that evening and told us that his brother had just come up from Tralee and that all was quiet down South. Dublin was alone in the fight! Later in the evening my sister, Eva, reported for duty to Commandant Pearse. Judge of my delight when a message was brought to me on the roof to say my sister was in and would like to see me. We saw each other for a few moments each day.

As night approached the fighting became more intense. We were able after some time to distinguish the different sounds of the guns. The Howth rifles sounded like small cannon compared with the modern rifle. It was easy to recognise the report of the shotguns and the rat-a-tat-tat of the machine guns. There were still crowds outside the G.P.O. and the number was increased by those returning from Fairyhouse Races. A number of Volunteers, thinking that the manoeuvres had been postponed indefinitely, had gone to the Races. Some, on returning to the city, joined up with their units or with the nearest group they could contact.

I need hardly say that we got no opportunity of sleeping on this our first night on the roof. As I lay on the sloping roof gazing up at the star-studded sky, my thoughts naturally turned to my loved ones at home. I knew how worried my parents would be when I I did not go home for the Easter vacation. However I put away these thoughts as much as I could lest they would interfere with that which had a greater claim to our love and loyalty. As dawn broke over the Bay of Dublin we resumed our watch on the Liffey.

Tuesday

I was still one of the group on duty on the roof. We were so excited the previous day that very little in the way of food satisfied us though there was no shortage of tea and bread and butter. On Tuesday meals were more regular as the kitchen staff were better organised. We went down at specified times for our meals. Desmond Fitzgerald seemed to be in charge of the commissariat department and at times we thought him very niggardly in dishing out the grub. He was evidently expecting a long sojourn in the G.P.O.

As I mentioned already, Brian Joyce and Eoghan Ó Briain were my companions in our section under the flag. Each night we said the Rosary and indeed at frequent intervals during the day. 'Twas not an unusual sight to see a Volunteer with his rifle grasped firmly in his hands and his Rosary beads hanging from his fingers. Eoghan Ó Briain 'gave out' the Rosary in our corner. He was much older than either Brian or I and was a married man with more responsibilities on his shoulders than we had. He couldn't stand any cursing or swearing or strong language. In this connection there was a famous character by the name of Jack White whose language was of the lurid style. He belonged to the Citizen Army and had been engaged by Commandant J. Connolly for special work and had afterwards re-joined him in the Post Office. One would have to see Jack in order to appreciate the stories about him. He was a seafaring man and, according to his own yarns, had seen the seamy side of life in many lands. A small sallow man, with ear-rings, you'd take him for a foreigner, certainly. His story of how he succeeded in cutting the head off of a Greek in one of his 'foreign encounters' thrilled us but his mode of expressing himself had poor Eoghan in a state of collapse almost.

Towards evening the fighting all around us was growing in intensity. The military were gradually closing in around the city. Shelling from a gun-boat on the Liffey commenced on the buildings around the G.P.O. Machine guns from the direction of Trinity

College and the Tivoli (now the offices of the *Irish Press*) were spraying bullets across O'Connell Street. By this time the crowds had melted away. The streets were deserted. We had a few men posted in buildings opposite the G.P.O. but we had not sufficient numbers to make a counter attack.

Wednesday

We were still in our corner on the roof but the position was becoming more and more dangerous. One never knew when an enemy sniper might find his target. Our snipers were busy too but for most of us 'twas a hidden enemy encircling our position. As a result of the shells from the Liffey gun-boat, fires had started all around us. I shall never forget the sight of Clery's in flames. We could feel the heat from our place on the roof. I remember Commandant Connolly coming around on this day to inspect our positions. He inspired us with great confidence by the cool calm attitude he adopted to the firing all around. He was a grand character and did everything he could for the comfort of his men. We were becoming, towards evening, rather weary from lack of sleep and the constant strain of watching and waiting for the attack was beginning to tell on us. That night, however, our group was replaced by others and we were brought down to the ground floor, where there were mattresses strewn just behind the front entrance to the building. Here we stretched our weary limbs and tried to sleep as best we could.

Thursday

I slept soundly enough but was awakened very early in the morning to take up duty again. This time, however, we were, stationed at the front and corner windows of the ground floor. I remember I was put at the corner facing towards O'Connell Bridge, but we would exchange positions now and then to relieve the monotony. Before going on duty we had a wash and then something to eat. The windows were well sandbagged with just a small opening for firing through. Most of the St Enda's boys were with me at this time. George Plunkett seemed to be the officer in command of this particular section.

I should have mentioned that on Monday evening we got news that a contingent of Volunteers from Maynooth had reached our Headquarters. I naturally was very anxious to meet anybody from Kildare and proud of the fact that my County was represented in the fight. I went down to meet them. Joe Buckley's father was with them. I was glad to get news of Joe who would have been with us only that he had to take his father's place at home, as the rest of the family were very young and his mother was an invalid. The Maynooth men were led to the city by Captain Tom Byrne, a man who had seen active service under Major John McBride in the Boer War of 1899–1900. On Tuesday the Maynooth men were sent over to strengthen our unit in the *Evening Mail* office.

Towards mid-day on Thursday our position in the G.P.O. became very serious. The fires had now extended from Clery's right down to Hopkins' corner and from the Metropole Hotel, the next building on our right, down to O'Connell's Bridge. In fact, the whole area was one mass of flames but the G.P.O. had not as yet caught fire But it was only a matter of time until this would also be on fire. Shells were constantly bursting on the roof and many of the Rathfarnham Company who had relieved us on Wednesday received facial wounds. All eventually were ordered down to the lower floors. We were ordered to build barricades further back from the front window. We were sent down to the coal cellars and ordered to fill bags with coal and carry them up to the ground floor. A foolish move, I thought afterwards, as coal would not prove very effective protection against bullets. However, 'twas all we had convenient. We worked like navvies for a good spell and then resumed our front line positions. What a change had come over the scene since Monday and Tuesday! Not a soul was to be seen, only a huge wall of flames towering to the sky and great billows of smoke. The noise of bursting shells and tumbling walls and roofs was indescribable. As one old soldier prisoner remarked, 'It was worse than Flanders.' Machine guns were still spraying the street with bullets. I saw one poor civilian rushing out in front of Nelson Pillar only to meet his death right in front of our window. By this time all our men had been withdrawn from their posts on the opposite side and brought back to the Post Office. It was miraculous that none of our men were shot whilst crossing backwards and forwards from Clery's to the G.P.O. It was necessary on one occasion for a party to go across for a supply of mattresses, etc. They got across safely but when returning they ran into a shower of bullets. One man tripped and fell with the mattress on top of him. He got up quite calmly, however, and got in without a scratch. I was wondering where Eva was all this time. It seems she had been sent across the other side of the street to Reis' shop to attend to some wounded men there. Captain Tom Weafer was killed while she was there. She was the last, I think, to be with him when he died. Not long afterwards the whole building took fire and she along with others of Cumann na mBan and garrison were brought back to the G.P.O. It was on this day also Commandant Connolly was wounded. He was lying on a stretcher at the back of the Post Office. Jim Ryan was the doctor in charge and he had the assistance of an English R.A.M.C. who was one of our prisoners.

Coming on towards dusk Captain George Plunkett asked Conor McGinley and myself to go with Paddy Weafer (Tom's brother) to help in boring through the houses in Henry Street in order that we might find a way of joining our comrades in the Four Courts. We set off in single file, Weafer leading the way. The poor fellow had just heard of his brother's death and he was greatly upset. On our way we passed Tom Clarke. He stopped us and shook hands with each of us. The three of us continued our way upstairs through walls already bored down 2nd floors and up to top floors, zig-zagging our way in the darkness through the Coliseum. I remember how weird and ghostly the auditorium of the Coliseum looked as we made our way through the gallery and on into the 'Wax Works'. I don't know how far up Henry Street we had gone when, 'Halt! Who goes there?' rang out. It was, of course, one of our own men whom we were to assist with the continuation of the boring. It appeared that we had reached the terminus of the boring operations and were told that no further movement in that direction was contemplated for the moment. It was late at this time, so Conor and I wrapped ourselves as best we could in the one overcoat; sat down on the floor with our backs to a wall and fell fast asleep. I remember awakening in the middle of the night – just as Commandant P.H. Pearse and two other officers were passing through on a tour of inspection.

Friday

Came the dawn and Conor and I woke up feeling very sore and stiff in every bone. We were anxious, seeing that no further boring was to be done, to get back to our own section on the ground floor of the G.P.O. I managed to get down to Commandant Pearse and asked him for a note ordering our transfer back to our own comrades. He readily gave me the necessary order and included the name of J.J. MacElligott who wished to be with us. I was one of the few whom J.J. knew in the G.P.O. He really should have reported to Jacob's Factory where his own Company were operating and where his cousin, Paddy Kelly, was but he was unable to reach there and had come into the G.P.O. We were both glad of one another's company. We got back without any difficulty, had a wash to take the sleep out of our eyes and resumed our posts at the windows. The place was now an inferno. Some of our men were hosing the flames that had spread along the roof and, between the flames, the smoke and the water dripping down on us, we didn't feel very comfortable. Still we made the welkin ring with rousing song and chorus, just to keep our spirits up. Soon we heard the sad news of The O'Rahilly's death. He had gone out at the head of a section to try to force an opening up Moore Street when he, with some others, were killed by machine gun fire. Amongst those killed with The O'Rahilly was Francis Macken, one of our own 'E' Company. He had a hairdressing establishment in Rathfarnham and came regularly to the College. He was a great little soldier and, as Section Commander in the Company, always gave the commands in Irish.

Owing to the seriousness of the position, the Cumann na mBan were sent with the wounded and the Red Cross section to Jervis Street Hospital. I had no opportunity of seeing my sister, Eva, before she went. About 2 o'clock in the afternoon all the Companies were ordered to line up in the yard of the G.P.O. in preparation for leaving the burning building. All the available food, including hams, bread, tinned food, etc., were collected in one place and a portion given to each man as he passed by. Jimmy Kenny (Terenure) and I, amongst others, were distributing the food. While thus engaged a shot rang out and, one man fell wounded. I cannot recall whether this man was J. Kenny or Dr Ted Kelly (Maynooth). Both were wounded at this time anyhow. I thought 'twas the beginning of an attack so I procured a 'gammon' and promptly took my place in the ranks. The retreat was carried out in a very orderly manner. There was no panic whatsoever. We marched out in two-deep, each man holding his rifle pointing upwards lest, in the closely packed formation, a rifle might go off accidentally.

I remember well. Bulfin was in front of me. When we reached the side door leading into Henry Street Commandant Pearse was standing in the small hallway watching and waiting until the last man had passed out of the building. As the street was being swept by machine gun fire from Mary Street direction, we had to make a dash across in one's and two's into Henry Lane. Bulfin made the journey with great speed. My turn was next. I thought my overcoat, to which I had the gammon fastened in front, might be an unnecessary burden and might possibly trip me as I ran, so I discarded both and threw them in a corner. I could see the bullets like hailstones hopping on the street and I thought that 'twould be a miracle to get to the other side scatheless. With head down as if running against heavy rain, I ran as I never ran before or since and got into Henry Lane without a scratch. The remarkable fact was that no one was hit while running this dangerous gauntlet.

When we got into Henry Lane all men with bayonets were ordered to the front. I was unfortunate in that I was the only one of the St Enda group to have a bayonet attached to my rifle. I never liked the idea of a bayonet charge as I always pictured myself being at the receiving end. There was nothing for it anyhow but to leave my comrades and go up to the front. Just at the bend of the lane, 'Commandant' [Sean] McLaughlin (who afterwards said he had been promoted to that rank 'on the field' by Commandant James Connolly) was roaring and shouting at us to 'charge the white house'. I'm blessed if I could see any white house but in company with the rest I charged. We had to pass a laneway which runs parallel with Moore Street down to Parnell Street. At the Parnell Street end there was a barricade from which the British were firing. We got by the lane opening safely, however, and it was then I saw the 'white house' indicated by our officer. It was at the corner of Moore Street and

Henry Lane. We broke in the door and found ourselves in a 'stone-beer' store. There was no enemy in waiting for us and for the moment we were out of the firing line. Bat Bourke, Paddy Donnelly and the Sweeney brothers, all of 'E' Company, were with me inside. We went upstairs and proceeded to barricade the windows on the instructions of a fine young Captain in full uniform. This was our first meeting with the famous Mick Collins. I don't think he was pleased with the way we had barricaded the windows but we could do no better as we had not the material at hand. Besides we were practically exhausted by this time from lack of food and sleep. 'Twas impossible to keep awake. As soon as one sat down; one's head began to nod over one's rifle. The only remedy was to try to keep on one's feet. After some time we got orders to leave the store and go into the house opposite. This house faced on to Moore Street and our men had bored their way through the houses until they reached a yard which opened out on the second lane in Moore Street near Parnell Street end.

What a queer life! Creeping through holes into bedrooms, then downstairs and through another opening into sitting-rooms, through shops, and finally to our resting place for the night near the above-mentioned yard (I think it belonged to Hanlon's). All was silence. We were under strict orders not to make any noise or to use our fire arms. The owners or occupiers of the houses seemed to have all gone away as we met with no opposition. All our men had got safely from the G.P.O. and were in silent occupation of the row of houses on this side of Moore Street (i.e., the right-hand side looking from Henry Street). The wounded Commandant Connolly was carried on a stretcher right through to a house about half-way up the street. Commandant Pearse and other officers were with him. We were completely surrounded. The military were entrenched behind a high barricade at the end of Moore Street. We could see from our windows dead bodies of civilians lying out on the path opposite. I took particular notice of one poor man with a white flag grasped in his hand, lying dead on the doorstep of his house. He had evidently been shot while evacuating his home for a safer place. We had a very patchy sleep that night as we suffered from the hunger and the thirst.

Saturday 29th April, 1916 The Surrender

...We learned that Commandant Pearse in consultation with Commandant Connolly and the other officers had decided that enough had been achieved to save Ireland's honour and 'that it was time to arrest the slaughter of the civilian population by British shells and bullets'. It was about 3 o'clock in the afternoon when the unconditional surrender took place. We were all called back to one of the larger rooms and there Seán Mac Diarmuda explained what Headquarters had decided to do and the reasons which compelled them to come to such a decision. He spoke with emotion of the fight against fearful odds by the Dublin Brigade, that they, the leaders, knew what fate awaited them but they hoped that the rank and file would be treated leniently. There were tears in his eyes as he was speaking.

Right Hon. Sir Alfred Bucknill, London, S.W.7. Deputy Judge Advocate General to the British Forces in Ireland in 1916.[5]

Letters of an English soldier in Ireland

My first scene in Dublin was one of civil war. We arrived in the very early hours of the morning and steamed up to North Wall, silent and dark. The Custom House stood out against a background of fire. There were at least four distinct fires burning, and great flames were leaping up in different places as if the whole city north of the Liffey was doomed. Occasionally one heard the crack of a rifle and the knocking of machine gun fire. We arrived at the quay and found a vessel lying alongside with a gun mounted in her bows. The crew of this vessel had left but there was one man on board in charge of the gun and he helped us to tie up alongside. A staff officer then came on board, an Irishman who was wearing the military cross ribbon earned in France. He was a man of invincible cheerfulness. 'Sure, we've had a fine fight' was his answer to all the questions thrust at him. After a while another staff officer arrived with two cars, and we got ashore on the quay, which had a primitive barricade of large barrels. After some delay in getting our luggage ashore we mounted

---

5 B.M.H., W.S. 1,019

the cars and drove away to Royal Hospital. It was impossible to go direct as the Four Courts and the Post Office were held by the rebels and there was no other way except to go round by the North Circular Road. We passed Liberty Hall, which had been shelled on the previous day, and then pursued a somewhat exciting course owing to the excessive vigilance of our picquets who challenged us almost every 50 yards. On one occasion the leading car did not pull up sufficiently quickly and three of a picquet had their rifles up to their shoulders. If that car had pulled up a few seconds later it would have most certainly have been perforated.

We arrived safely at Royal Hospital about 3 a.m. on 28/4/16 (Friday), and after a cup of tea went to bed for a few hours. I cannot remember that anything exciting happened on the Friday. We had a sentry patrolling the little wall running between the garden and the drive and he occasionally had a shot at something, what I never discovered. There was also another sentry who patrolled along the embankment behind the wall looking towards the Dublin Union. I looked over this wall and could see very distinctly the Republican green flag hanging from one of the windows of the Union. General Maxwell threw out a hint that someone might like to earn two guineas by bringing the flag in, but it remained there so far as I know until the surrender on the Sunday. There were a good many troops quartered at the hospital and they slept in the corridors. There was also a divisional train picketed in the field looking towards Kilmainham Gaol on the N[orth] side of the avenue. I wandered about the house on Friday morning and found a bullet mark on the wall of the drawing-room, which had come through the window apparently from the direction of Park Gate.

On Saturday morning I was busy drafting a paper for General Byrne and after lunch went down with him to Parkgate. Whilst we were there, we heard that probably the whole affair was over, and shortly afterwards Pearse the rebel leader arrived and saw General Maxwell. Pearse surrendered immediately and sent out notices to his followers to do the same. I saw this man later on in the day at Arbour Hill Barracks where he was removed. I went there with General Byrne. Pearse was dressed in green uniform with yellow stare tabs and he had a hat rather like a Colonial's with one side turned up. He was tall and well set up, with high cheek bones and eyes deep set. I remember that he said he had brought some money with him to pay for his food and he requested that he might have special food, but this request was not then granted.

It was obvious from the commencement that there would be great difficulty in getting sufficient legal evidence to pin any particular offence against any particular person, and that the only thing to do was to get the names of officers who could identify prisoners as having taken part in the fighting and having surrendered with arms in their hands. In talking with an officer, a Sec[ond] L[eftenan]t Watson of the Royal Irish Rifles, who was in charge of a detachment of men at Royal Hospital, I found that he had been engaged in the fighting at the Dublin Union and had helped to take a good many prisoners there who were now at Kilmainham. I told General Byrne this, who arranged with H.Q. that the evidence of this officer should be taken, but nothing was done, and on the Monday I went to Kilmainham and took a summary myself of his evidence in the case of various men whom he and other men in his Company identified.

The prisoners that I saw then were in rather a deplorable state. Some of them had been wounded and they all looked dirty and unkempt. I was very surprised to hear two of them, Beazley and Duggan say they were solicitors. The leader at the Union was Kent [Eamonn Ceannt], who was not taken prisoner by Mr Watson, but several of the prisoners said that he was in command there. A man called Irvine, a secondary school teacher, was second in command. I gathered from most of the statements made by the accused that they had no knowledge on the Monday morning that there was going to be a rebellion until they were suddenly rushed in to the South Union gate at the double and taken in to the huts where the fighting took place, where they were told to barricade themselves as they were about to be attacked by the military. This was their version. It is undoubtedly true that some of the company or battalion of the Irish Volunteers who were taken to the South Dublin Union lined the hedge on the left side of the road and ambushed the Royal Irish Regiment who were marching down to the Castle and killed several of them. The Irish, as I was told by officers there, hadn't the slightest idea of what they were in for, and were marching along in fours when they were fired on. They then doubled back under cover and attacked across the fields in open order whilst another party worked their way round to the canal side and attacked there. They then stormed the huts, where they found the rebels mixed up with the patients and a most horrible confusion.

I never heard that any man was tried for firing on the troops in this ambush. So far as I know no rebels captured in the Union was executed. Irvine, the most prominent man captured there, was sentenced to ten years' penal servitude.

On Sunday (April 30th) a large number of rebels surrendered and they were brought up to Richmond Barracks. I saw the Countess Markievicz arrive there at the head of her company. When I saw her she was standing gnawing an orange in the barrack square with a number of young women prisoners standing behind her. She was dressed in dark green knickerbockers and puttees and tunic and had a green hat with cock's feathers in it. I saw her again on another day when she was brought to Richmond Barracks from Kilmainham for a summary of evidence to be taken. She was brought over in a motor ambulance attended by a wardress and a guard of soldiers. I took the summary of evidence in her case, and from the statement of a page-boy at a hotel facing Stephen's Green it appeared that he saw her fire her revolver at a window in the hotel from which an officer in uniform was looking out. The bullet struck the window sill. When I asked her whether she wished to say anything, she said 'We dreamed of an Irish Republic and thought we had a fighting chance.' Then for a few moments she broke down and sobbed.

Pearse, MacDonagh and Clarke were tried on the first day that the court sat and were all condemned to death and executed on the following morning at Kilmainham Gaol. Pearse during the time of waiting before his trial had written a letter from prison to his mother which was used in evidence against him at his trial. This letter is now attached to the proceedings in his case and is interesting because he says there 'I have reason to believe that the German expedition on which I counted actually set sail but was defeated by the British fleet.' Pearse appears to have been a very considerable orator. I was told that he was really a wonderful speaker. He made the funeral oration at the burial of O'Donovan Rossa at Glasnevin Cemetery in

1915. I saw him saluted by some of his men who were also waiting trial in a very respectful manner. One of the Royal Irish officers told me that after the rebels had been driven out of the Post Office by the fire raging there, they collected in the side Street by the Coliseum and seemed uncertain what to do and then Pearse came up and spoke to them and in a few minutes they were cheering and rushed after him in the direction of Moore St. Pearse made an appeal to General Maxwell to spare the lives of his followers if he forfeited his own life. I had to hand Pearse General Maxwell's letter in reply but do not know its contents.

I believe from what those who were present at his execution told me that these three men and indeed all who were executed died bravely. MacDonagh indeed came down the stairs whistling. They were blindfolded in a passage and had a piece of paper pinned on their coats over the heart and were then led out. They were shot at two different spots in two different yards in the gaol. I saw the places of execution. They could not be overlooked from any windows, but the noise must have been terrific. It frightened the people living near who thought it was artillery. Each firing party had twelve men, and the executions took place at 3.45 a.m. At first I used to sleep very badly at Royal Hospital because I could not help thinking of these unfortunate men dying not more than ¼ mile away, and on the first occasion I heard the march of the firing party going out from Royal Hospital but I never heard the firing. I believe that P.H. Pearse did not see his mother before his execution because the motor which was sent for her was stopped by the picquets and could not get through. Every arrangement was made to get the relatives to the gaol on the night before the executions, and a priest was always in attendance at the execution and burial. A large grave was dug at Arbour Hill Detention Barracks and the bodies were removed there for burial.

❧

Desmond Ryan, Lieut. Dublin Brigade, Irish Volunteers, 1916.[6]

In the summer of 1915 I went on a holiday to Rosmuck with Pearse and his brother and I had a good many conversations with him. He was more open in his speech than I had ever known him to be. He was getting ready for the O'Donovan–Rossa funeral. Anyway we went back to Dublin and were at this funeral. He knew I was going on to Donegal so he asked me how long I'd be away. This brings me to the autumn of 1915. So he told me that if I got a message from him or from his sister or from Eamonn Ceannt asking for a certain book I was to return at once because there would be a fight in Dublin that day. That is the autumn of 1915. Well I got no order and Pearse never referred to that again.

You are aware, of course, that Connolly was pressing Pearse very hard for action and that he was very worried about Connolly though he said afterwards to John Kilgannon and Peter Slattery who had been talking to him, 'The trouble is I have been holding people in that I really agreed with.' That was his attitude. The nearer it got to 1916 the more cute and careful Pearse became. We all felt there was a Rising coming. The nearer it got the more he shut up. In January, 1916, – 22nd and 29th – Pearse asked me one night in the Hermitage

---

[6] B.M.H., W.S. 725

'Had I got it?'. This was in reference to the *Workers' Republic* which he knew I got. Then he read it very carefully. He said to me, 'That is dangerous enough'. Then he told me that he had not been able to sleep for a week; the Citizen Army were threatening action and that he and Seán MacDermott had gone to Connolly, told him they were going to have a Rising, that he was ruining their plans and would he hold his hand. Finally Pearse persuaded Connolly. He said there seemed to be a terrible mental struggle going on in Connolly at the time and then with tears in his eyes he (Connolly) grasped Pearse's hand and said, 'God grant, Pearse, that you were right', and Pearse said, 'God grant that I was.' Pearse added to me, 'Perhaps Connolly was right; he is a very great man.' He said nothing about kidnapping or anything like that. I have covered this fully in my book on the Rising on the Connolly kidnapping in the appendix to the second edition. In the spring of 1914, Pádraig Pearse and Bulmer Hobson visited the United States with introductions from Clarke and MacDermott recommending Pearse. Pearse made a tour for the school as well as for his other work. He was helped very much by [John] Devoy and the Clan [na Gael] and Irish organisations generally. Devoy said if he had stayed he would have raised all the money he wanted. Another point on that which worried Pearse very much: there was a kind of conflict between sacrificing the school for his Volunteer principles and ideals. He said the only time you can rise is in a time similar to the Boer War when there were few troops in the country and the enemy was otherwise engaged. On a couple of occasions in 1915–26 we did discuss the question of a Rising or not. 'Consider how would we look', said Pearse, and what would the people think of us after all our talk and promises if we said, 'Well, after all the British are too strong and we don't feel like fighting them. The people would just laugh at us and our movements would collapse in laughter.' Pearse thought his speeches and conduct had committed him to action. In 1913 when the Volunteers were founded, he said to me, 'We started a Rising to-night.'

Pearse had a great respect for MacNeill but complained that he was 'a Grattan come to life again'. He could never make up his mind. Pearse thought Connolly was unjust in some of his criticisms of both MacNeill and Hobson but said neither of them was revolutionary.

His relations with Hobson from 1912 down to the acceptance of the Redmond ultimatum in June 1914, were friendly and he always spoke with respect of Hobson's motives. He was quite prepared, to my mind, to fight Redmond on the nominee question but was relieved when it was decided to give way to Redmond for the moment. He later blamed Hobson for the admission of the nominees, and their relations were not so friendly from that time. I did not know Hobson was arrested until I heard it during the Rising but there was a great friend of Hobson, Seán Lester – later prominent as a League of Nations officer – who told me the story too, that Hobson was summoned to a meeting in Martin Conlon's house in Phibsboro' and when he got there he met some 'friends' of his who produced revolvers and arrested him. I think Hobson was not really surprised. Pearse once told me that he sent for the Germans, that they were bringing arms and ammunition. I think that may have been in March 1915 or perhaps late in 1915. He said in a kind of gay manner, 'I have sent for the Germans.' 'Are they sending troops?' 'Oh, no, they are coming in aeroplanes and sending arms and ammunition.' In regard to a general plan for the Rising in Easter Week, I heard Pearse say, 'Plans were concealed in the form of a novel.' I identified that novel for some reason or other with Joseph Plunkett. I did know there were certain documents in St. Enda's which Pearse was very worried about. One day he went out with his brother and all the boys and he asked me, 'Are you stopping in?' So I was and he said, 'If any 'G' man comes, shoot him; fire a shot and kill him.' Miss Pearse talked about certain documents which were there and if discovered would lead to people being hanged. I asked her about that when I came back to Ireland in 1939 and she said she had completely forgotten. For some months before the Rising, I helped in the manufacture of tin-can hand grenades and the filling of shotgun cartridges in the Hermitage, Rathfarnham, a work which was spread over three months, to the best of my recollection. I believe we made about 500 canister bombs. This work was undertaken at the request of P.H. Pearse, and was done under the directions of Peter Slattery, then a Science Master in St. Enda's, and carried out by Eamonn Bulfin, 1st Lieutenant of E. Coy, 4th Battalion; Fintan Murphy; Joseph Sweeney; Frank Burke; Brian Joyce; Connor MacGinley; and for a fortnight before the Rising by Liam Mellows. Part of our work was the hiding of Mellows after his escape from internment in England. We saw him off from the Hermitage on the Thursday before Easter Week. We were all trusted implicitly by P.H. Pearse, and as regards the Rising he told us everything except the date, although as I have said, he grew rather subtle towards the end, and we were never quite sure. Once we were visited by Seán MacDermott, and Pearse said, as apparently Seán MacDermott was visiting the place more or less secretly: 'You can trust these. They won't talk'. Pearse handed over Mellows to our care when Mellows came disguised as a priest. When raids for ammunition became frequent before the Rising about 1915, Pearse made us carry around several hundred rounds of .303 concealed on our persons all day, on trams, in the streets, everywhere till the alarm died down.

The grenades were stored in a room in the basement of St Enda's, and our work on the bombs was carried out in our study room – we were all N[ational] U[niversity] [of] I[reland] students in an upper room of the Hermitage. We did a good deal of breaking of scrap iron to fill the grenades, which were mainly canisters – a matchbox filled with an explosive made of permanganate of potash, phosphorus, etc., and ignited by a fuse. (This was all the work of Peter Slattery who injured himself once when an explosion occurred in the Science Lab, where he made up the explosive). Another part of our work was the making of batons for use against looters.

On Easter Sunday night the last load of these grenades were removed to Liberty Hall or Kimmage or both probably. Dr Kathleen Lynn drove them in her car, accompanied by Eamonn Bulfin. Later the same night Pearse sent me with a written message to Connolly whom I met in his small room in Liberty Hall. He just nodded, said it would be all right as he would meet Pearse later. There was an armed guard outside his door. Earlier on Easter Saturday I brought a letter to Seán T. O'Kelly from Pearse, asking whether Sean T. could put Pearse and his brother up for the night. [The text of this letter is given in Le Roux's *Life of Pearse*, pp. 366–7.] Seán T. O'Kelly read the letter, nodded and smiled, and told me to tell Pearse that 'that would be all right'. He may have written a reply too. Pearse and his brother left St Enda's that evening.

They returned on Easter Sunday afternoon. I never saw Pearse so silent and disturbed. He simply could not speak to anyone. Willie Pearse told me the same thing. We had all spent a sleepless Saturday night, all ready for the events of Sunday, then came the news of the MacNeill countermand in the Sunday Independent. 'That', said Willie, very sadly, 'was a most dangerous hint to the military that something was in the wind'. Then the two brothers went off quietly. We all felt it was a crisis; that the whole movement was in the balance; that everything might now collapse. It was a most extraordinary feeling, very strong, yet hard to define. Anyone who lived through the time must know it well, and it always comes back when arguments arise as to the rights or wrongs of the Rising of 1916. We felt that at any moment a spring, the spring of the whole Irish–Ireland movement might snap, and nothing would ever in our lifetimes mend it again. Yet it seemed as if the whole chance of striking first had gone, and we talked and talked round it. It was the beginning of a curious feeling that we were in a dream.

About ten o'clock on Easter Monday morning, Pearse sent special messages, scribbled on small pages of a note book to Eamonn Bulfin, to Joseph Sweeney and to me, telling us to inform all in St Enda's – about eleven of us or so were concerned – to carry out the mobilisation order, and to remove all remaining guns and ammunition, etc. from St Enda's.

❋

A Rebel's Tale: Easter Week in the G.P.O. by Dick Humphreys.

Easter Monday, 1916, Noon

Suddenly through the lovely summer-like air of that fatal bank holiday two shots ring out reverberatingly. Then follows a machine-gun-like succession of reports, and finally an immense explosion. People stop on the footpaths and look questionably at one another. A very few straightaway realise what has happened, and become the centres of chattering crowds. All at once one notices that a great silence, terrible in its unnaturalness, has fallen on the city. Then again come those foreboding shots, seven or eight whipping out viciously the imperial summons of the god Mars. Two policemen run up from the Stephen's Green direction and scurry into Lad Lane. Some queer feeling in the air prevents one from wholly realising the utter ridiculousness of their action. At the moment one seems capable of unmovably watching the most grotesque thing. A valiant sergeant suddenly makes his appearance, and proceeds to stop all inward-bound cars. One motor driver remonstrates indignantly, disdainfully daring anyone to stop him. Later on his car was seen picturesquely placed at one end of the Shelbourne barricade. At Stephen's Green (East) a large and ever-increasing crowd had collected rumours of Hun-like atrocities abound on all sides. Nevertheless the self-same crowd seems to have a strange confidence in those 'Huns', considering that barely the width of a street separates them. Save for the complete absence of holiday-makers, and the barred gates, indeed, one would notice nothing unusual on glancing inside the Park.

* * *

Tension grows throughout the afternoon. Crowds throng around the different positions. Everyone is waiting for the supposed coming advance of the military. Then suddenly rumour has it that the Germans have been seen on the North side. One old lady informs me gratuitously in Westmoreland Street that a 'corpse of Germans' has landed in the Park, whether from warships or Zeppelins not stated. Likewise she adds that the Sinn Féiners have set up a courthouse in the G.P.O. At O'Connell Street I finally learn that Ireland has been proclaimed a Republic. Slates of broken glass lying on the Pavement outside attract gruesome crowds. They look just like pools of crimson blood. The numbers of onlookers in O'Connell Street and around the G.P.O. is truly stupendous. It takes me fully twenty minutes to get as far as the Metropole Hotel…

Wednesday morning finds things beginning to get lively. Bullets are pattering on the walls and windows of the Imperial, Reis's, the D.B.C., Hopkins, etc., all of which are held by us. An ever inquisitive crowd is standing in D'Olier Street and O'Connell Bridge, right between the two firing parties. They appear quite unconcerned. Indeed, one would think from their appearance that the whole thing was merely a sham battle got up for their amusement. Towards ten o'clock, however, they gradually disappear, and half an hour later the streets shine bare in the sunlight.

For the next few hours we work hard, rendering our section of the defences (the east room) as bullet-proof as possible. Stationary presses are raided, and a wall of notebooks six or seven feet deep is built inside the window. Then follows a line of sacks full of coal, all the sand having been utilised in the lower storeys. To prevent these rather inflammable materials caching fire the whole place is drenched by means of one of the large firing hoses. Four loopholes have been left in the barricade, through which we place our rifles. There follows an unexciting vigil during which we watch the empty streets unceasingly. Our window commands O'Connell Street from the Imperial Hotel to Carlisle Building and the fire station on the opposite side of the Liffey. Intermittent fire is going on on all [sides], but, save for the occasional spent bullet, our building is not touched as yet.

About 2 o'clock p.m. a gigantic boom shakes the edifice to its foundations, and everyone looks up with startled eye. From all sides come questioning words. Some say that a bomb has exploded in the lower room. Others that it is a dynamite explosion, but a second and third in quick succession prove the correctness of those who proclaimed it heavy artillery. The detonations are truly tremendous, and were we not absolutely certain that the gun was situated on the opposite side of the river, one could have sworn that it was at least in Abbey Street. For a time the men are uneasy at this their first experience of heavy gun-fire, but soon they become quite accustomed to the sound, and take no more notice of it than of the ordinary rifle fire. About 4 o'clock we learn that Kelly's shop has been shelled and its defenders forced to retire. A machine-gun has meantime been placed on the Brunswick St. Fire Station, and a hail of bullets begins to speckle the walls of the Imperial. Another one situated somewhere near Trinity College raises little rippling clouds of mortar from the front facade of the D.B.C. No. 1 is then turned on the G.P.O. It sounds like a sudden burst of hail against the ceiling. Our roofsnipers can command practically every point within range of the building, and they soon silence the machine-guns. Firing is still brisk on the west side, where the military are shooting from the Rotunda direction.

Towards six o'clock, however, the uproar gradually subsides, and for a few hours there is a local silence. About ten o'clock we suddenly noticed a well-dressed, middle-aged man coming up to O'Connell Bridge from the direction of Butt Bridge. The light of the electric arc lamps shine on his carefully-brushed tall hat. Both sides shout to him to get away. He seems dazed, and walks uncertainly for a few minutes. Suddenly a volley rings out from D'Olier Street, and he jumps about four feet into the air. Then with another bound he reaches the corner of the bridge and rushes down Eden Quay at racing pace. There seems something unreal about the thing. Seen in the unnatural light from the street standards, one cannot imagine it to be real live drama. Suddenly an officer enters the room. He orders three or four crack shots to smash the arc lamps. A few seconds later O'Connell Street is plunged into darkness. Only the stars shed a mystic glare over the house-tops.

Sleeping accommodation, as far as the rank and file are concerned, is pretty nonexistent. When our 'off-duty' turn arrives we hunt around for a reasonably quiet spot where we might snatch a short sleep. But despite its huge size the G.P.O. seems to possess no amenities of this kind and the best most of us can do is to bed down under a table, or desk, with a top cover thrown over us in lieu of the normal sheet or blanket. Needless to say no-one gets much sleep. The short intervals of silence outside are even more ominous in their eerie intensity than the shots, explosions, strange whistling and odd bursts of patriotic song which punctuate the night.

* * *

Thursday, April 27th, 6 A.M

It is a glorious day again with a burning sun glowing in a cloudless blue sky. A sullen rumble of heavy shooting from 'Jacob's' direction vibrates on the cool breeze like the rattle of a deadly snake. At the O'Rahilly's orders we spend the morning constructing imitation barricades in every window which opens outwards. This work necessitates the breaking in of numerous locked doors. The building seems immense. The number of separate rooms in the place is unbelievable. Meantime the bombardment has recommenced. Hopkins', the D.B.C., and the Imperial being under continuous fire, while the G.P.O. is subject to much sniping. The everlasting wait for the unexpected is terribly nerve-racking. Machine-guns stutter irregularly from all sides and add to the growing uproar.

Towards 3 o'clock we learn that there is going to be an attack from the North-west side. All the available men, therefore, are withdrawn from the eastern posts, and take up positions at the western windows. The excitement grows intense. Everyone is waiting. Suddenly rumour has it that an armoured car is approaching up Henry Street. Men show themselves insanely at the window to obtain a view. Then comes a tremendous explosion rising high above the rattle of rifle and machine-gun fire. The shooting dies down all at once, and there is a lull.

Pearse takes this opportunity of speaking to the men. His words consist of a short resume of events since the Monday morning. He commences by saying that K. has succeeded in overturning the armoured car with a bomb. 'All our principal positions,' he continues, 'are still intact. Commandant Daly has captured the Linenhall Barracks, taken two officers and twenty-three men prisoners, and set fire to he building. The country is steadily rising, and a large band of Volunteers is marching from Dundalk on Dublin. A successful engagement between a large body of police and an inferior number of Volunteers has taken place near Lusk, between thirty or forty police being captured. Barracks have been raided throughout the country, and especially in the Counties Dublin and Meath Wexford has risen and a relief column, to be marched on Dublin, is being formed. A large store of food supplies has been discovered in the building which will enable us to hold out till reinforcements from the country arrive and release us.'

He concludes by saying that we have now successfully held out as a Republic against the might of England for three full days. Wherefore, according to International law, we are legally entitled to the status of Republicanists and the presence of a delegate in that Peace Conference which must inevitably follow the war.

His words are answered by a deafening outburst of cheering which spreads throughout the whole building. Needless to say, this account puts new vitality into the men which three days' uncertainty and suspense had rather dispersed.

3.45 P.M.

The military commence shelling us in real earnest, and shrapnel shells begin to drop on the roof in quick succession. Two howitzers have been mounted near Findlater's Church. For ten or fifteen minutes our roof-snipers stand the fire, but begin to suffer heavily, three being wounded severely. Word to evacuate this position is accordingly given, and a minute later they come tumbling down through the safety man-holes into the telegraph room. These man-holes are just rough spaces torn in the slates and mortar through which a rope stretches down to the floor. Some of the men in their hurry fail to catch the rope altogether, and take the eighteen foot drop as though it were an everyday occurrence. The wounded are lowered safely by means of two ropes. This cannonade continues for about two and a half hours, but the shells, the majority of which seem to be shrapnel, fail to do any serious damage to our position. Snipers on the Gresham [Hotel], however, are sending a fusillade of bullets in through the western windows, and we are ordered to keep under cover as much as possible. We allow them to continue firing till, mystified at our silence, they grow bolder, and incautiously show themselves over the top of the parapet. Immediately a single volley rings out. There is no more sniping that evening from the Gresham.

The continuous 'boom' of the Howth guns echoing from all sides of the building show that the military are at length beginning to show themselves, but towards seven o'clock the cannonade slackens, and finally subsides to an occasional report now and again. The G.P.O., Imperial, Reis's, and all our minor posts are still intact.

7.30 P.M.

The surplus men return to their former positions in the eastern rooms, where the single guards have spent a most uninteresting and nerve-shattering evening listening to the firing all round them, but seeing nothing tangible. Hopkins is just beginning to blaze, while somewhere down in Abbey Street a thin column of smoke is rising into the still evening air. Not realising that this is the commencement of that huge conflagration which is to devastate O'Connell Street, we watch the leaping flame while gradually night darkens over the city.

On returning to our posts after tea we are appalled at the stupendous increase the fire has made. The interior of our room is as bright as day with the lurid glow of the flames. Reis's jewellery shop is a mass of leaping scarlet tongues of light. Behind it huge mountains of billowing jet black smoke are rolling up into the heavens. A roaring as of a gigantic waterfall re-echoes from the walls. Hopkins is completely hidden from view by a curtain of skimmering, hissings sparks. Up through the everchanging haze of smoke and flame, lifting itself proudly like one who scorns to notice the taunts of an enemy, rises the tower of the D.B.C. Ringed round with fire it stands undaunted while overhead the very sky quivers with the simmering heat. It seems symbolical of Ireland. Suddenly some oil works near Abbey Street is singed by the conflagration, and immediately a solid sheet of blinding, death-white flame rushes hundreds of feet into the air with a thunderous explosion that shakes the walls. It is followed by a heavy bombardment as hundreds of drums of oil explode. The intense light compels one to close the eyes. Even here the light is so terrible that it strikes one like a solid thing as blasts of scorching air come in through the glassless windows. Millions of sparks are floating in impenetrable masses for hundreds of yards around O'Connell Street, and as a precaution we are ordered to drench the barricades with water again. The whole thing seems too terrible to be real. Crimson-tinged men moved around dazedly. Above it all the sharp crackle of rifle fire predominates, while the deadly rattle of the machine-gun sounds like the coughing laughter of jeering spirits.

Gradually the fire spreads along O'Connell Street, and from a hissing murmur the sound grows to a thunderous booming, like the song of a great dynamo. Awe-stricken, the men gather together at the different posts and discuss the outbreak in hoarse whispers. 'How will it end?' 'Will it reach the Imperial?' 'Will the Post Office catch fire?' 'Is the whole city doomed?' Such are some of the questions that pass from lip to lip.

Suddenly an armoured car appears in Westmoreland Street. It moves towards us, and seems about to advance, but reverses instead, and disappears in the direction of Dame St. A shout rings out from the Imperial Hotel, and we see a figure standing at one of the windows. He makes a trumpet of his hands, and in clear tones informs us that the building has caught fire at the rear. He asks for further orders, and is told to get his men across to the G.P.O. if possible. Five minutes later four Volunteers are seen at the door of the Hotel. They signal to open the main door downstairs, and rush across the street in turns. From their windows we watch their passage breathlessly.

Ten minutes later the Imperial, together with the buildings on either side, is well ablaze, while over in the Henry Street direction another fire has broken out. We seem to be situated in the midst of a circle of flame. Inside the central telegraph room, which runs along the whole length of the G.P.O., the men standing silently at their posts, black and bronze statues against the terrible glare of the sky Unawed and undaunted, their gaze ever fixed on the glistening cobbles and shadowed lanes whence all attacks must be directed, they wait expectantly. Now and again the flames beat upwards in a flesh of light that reveals every detail behind the barriers, then they subside as suddenly, and lines of black shadows, rays of darkness, as it were, creep over us. Fortunately the wind is blowing seawards, and the myriads of blazing fragments are carried away from the G.P.O. Glowing sparks, however, now begin to shower down with a pattering like soft rain, and threaten to set everything on fire. All bombs and hand grenades are taken to the centre of the building, and again we drench barricades, walls and floors. Even in the midst of this inferno we are sniped at by the enemy, and occasional bullets com in through the windows. Clouds of dirty grey smoke prevent us from replying.

At about 12.30 the two Pearses, The O'Rahilly and some other officers make a tour of our defences. They seem quite satisfied as to the progress of things.

* * *

Friday, April 28th, The Fifth Day of the Irish Republic

The weather is sunny and fine as usual. On the opposite side of O'Connell Street nothing is left of the buildings save the bare walls. Clouds of grey smoke are wreathing around everywhere, and it is difficult to see as far as the Bridge. Occasionally some side wall or roof falls in with a terrific crash. The heat is stupefying, and a heavy odour of burning cloth permeates the air. All the barbaric splendour that night had lent the scene has now faded away, and the pitiless sun illuminates the squalidness and horror of the destruction. The morning is fairly quiet, but occasional shots ring out from the direction of the Four Courts. After breakfast we again take up our positions at the windows. The morning passes uneventfully in our area. We hear that Maxwell has arrived in Dublin. Towards twelve o'clock the smoke clears away from Hopkins's corner, and a machine-gun opens fire on our windows. From then on till 3 o'clock the shooting increases on all sides, the report of the Howth guns sounding more like artillery than rifles. About 3.30 p.m. a differently-noted fusillade rings out from the Gresham Hotel direction, and, to our astonishment, the side of the walls where the bullets lodge seem to flash into flame. Finding no hold, however, they became immediately extinguished. A minute or so later someone discovers that the roof is on fire, and immediately commences a perfect babble of shouting, order-giving and talking. The two main lines of hose are quickly brought to the spot, and two streams of water are thrown against the lower part of the roof. Lines of buckets are also organised, and after a quarter of an hour's hard work the outbreak seems to be practically under control. Suddenly another part of the roof is set on fire by the incendiary bullets, and half the available water supply has to be turned upon it. Heavy firing is meantime going on in all directions, and adds to the confusion. Pearse and J. Plunkett hold a short conversation at the doorway. They both appear very excited. Finally a large number of men are selected for extinguishing work, and the remainder are ordered to the windows. Everyone seems to consider it his duty to give orders at the top of his voice. The noise is terrific. The fire is gaining ground like lightning.

The O'Rahilly comes into the room. He is as cool as ever, one of the very few officers at this moment who really keeps his head. We are ordered to bring all bombs, spare rifles and loose ammunition down to the yard of the G.P.O. This done, we return to the windows again.

From our posts we can see right down along the telegraph room. It presents a most extraordinary spectacle. In one part the fire has eaten right through the roof, and slates and mortar are commencing to fall on the floor. The two hoses are brought to bear on this spot. They are held six feet above the ground (to enable a better head of water to be obtained) by lines of men. Here and there the water spurts out through small holes in the rubber, drenching the men completely. In one place a huge leak from a faulty connection runs down the uniform of an officer. In a few seconds he is wet to the skin, but stands as unconcernedly as though on parade. Further over a line of buckets extending down to the second floor is working with incredible rapidity.

After a few minutes, however, we see that all is useless. The fire is gaining ground in all directions. Huge masses of the roof commence to fall inwards with terrific noise. The floor on which the men are working threatens to give way with each blow. Clouds of smoke from the burning debris writhe around the corridors and passages. It gets into our eyes and noses, and compels fits of coughing. The floors are covered to a depth of three inches with grimy water.

From the yard below comes a noise of shouting, pulling about of bales and packages, and the thunderous report of the Howth rifles. We are warned to be ready for an attack at any moment. A thick pall of smoke has come down over O'Connell Street again, and we are unable to see beyond the corners of the Imperial Hotel. Ten or twelve minutes pass anxiously. The noise below increases in intensity.

The fire has practically demolished the whole telegraphic room, and is threatening every moment to cut off our retreat. O'Rahilly again appears, comes over, and tells me to join Desmond FitzGerald down in the restaurant. The G.P.O. is about to be evacuated. With a cheerful wave of his hand, and a smile, he steps quickly down the smoke-filed stairs. Little did I know that this would be the last time I would ever see him alive. Suddenly we hear a great cheer from somewhere beneath, followed by the quick beat of doubling footsteps. A sudden fusillade seems to burst out on all sides. Two or three machine-guns cough threateningly. The first party has left the G.P.O.

* * *

The further history of the defence of the G.P.O. area is a tragic one. An attempt is made to reach Williams and Woods' Factory, in order to use it as a base. It is soon discovered, however, that the military are massed in far too great a force along the Parnell Street district to render this plan possible. A body of select rifle men are, nevertheless, picked out, and with The O'Rahilly at their head a gallant charge is made at the barricades. On reaching the corner of the lane they come under the point-blank fire of a hidden machine gun. Practically every member of the little band is hit, The O'Rahilly and two others being wounded mortally.

Sniping continues all through the night. Though the men are scattered between the various buildings between Parnell Street and Henry Street, the military are still afraid to advance in force. All night long the fire gains ground. The G.P.O. is now nothing but an empty shell. The Coliseum [Theatre] and the Metropole are rapidly being reduced to ruins. Arnott's [shop] is already licked by the devouring flames. Overhead the quivering sky reflects the angry crimson of this furnace. It looks like a pall of blood. The ever-changing roaring sounds like the shrieks of a thousand demons. So our last night of freedom passes. Everyone seems to realise that our chances at length are hopeless. Without a central base, and completely isolated from our other strong-points and garrisons, how is it possible to hold out longer?

* * *

Saturday, April 29th

Saturday morning finds desultory shooting still going on. Headquarters' staff holds a long consultation in the office of a small shop. A conditional surrender is decided upon. Negotiations and an armistice go on from one till four o'clock. Then comes the fateful surrender. We are convinced, however, that an absolutely unconditional surrender was not agreed to. Arms are given up near the Rotunda and the men examined. A section is made of the wounded and marched to the Castle at the point of the bayonet. The remainder lie on the grass inside the Rotunda railings. No covering or food whatsoever is given them throughout the night.

Áine Ceannt,
Co. Dublin.[7]

In 1914 on the formation of Cumann na mBan I joined the Central Branch, the first to be established. After the Rising of 1916 I was appointed Honorary Treasurer and later one of the four Vice-Presidents, which rank I held until I retired in 1924. In 1917 I attended as a delegate at Count Plunkett's Convention. In October of the same year I was co-opted a member of the Standing or Executive Committee of Sinn Féin and was elected annually until I retired in 1924. In January, 1916, the Military Council started to meet in Eamonn Ceannt's house in Dolphin's Barn. Only on the first occasion did I meet the Council, and I then met Clarke, McDermott and Pearse. I have no recollection of meeting Joe Plunkett at that meeting, although he was probably there. Shortly after that meeting James Connolly disappeared.

I remember – I would say it would be about the end of the month of January or February, pay time in the Corporation – saying to Eamonn jocosely, 'Give me some money before the Rebellion starts.' Eamonn replied, 'It may start sooner than you expect.' Then he added, 'James Connolly has disappeared.' Connolly had instructed his next-in-command that if at any time he disappeared and did not turn up within three days the Citizen Army was to go out and take Dublin Castle. Eamonn said, 'We can't let the Citizen Army go out

[7] B.M.H., W.S. 264

alone, if they go out we must go with them. Three of us are going to see [Michael] Mallin to ask him to hold his hand.' I think Eamonn said McDermott was one, but I am not sure of the names of the three. Eamonn said, 'I am going now to see what was the result of the deputation that went over to the Citizen Army, asking them to wait a few days. In the meantime I have ordered all the officers of the Fourth Battalion to report here, and on my return it will be either to give them orders for ordinary manoeuvres, if the situation has cleared, or, alternatively, to tell them their places for the fight.' When he returned, at about half-past ten, he dismissed the men rather quickly and told me that Connolly had re-appeared.

At the next meeting of the Military Council, held at our house, Connolly was present and was a member of that body from that day forward. On 17th March, 1916, the Dublin Battalions, up to two thousand strong, were inspected by Eoin MacNeill at College Green. They had assembled at St Michael's and John's Church for a special military Mass at nine o'clock. On this occasion the honour of serving the Mass and of providing the Guard of Honour for presenting arms at the Elevation was given to the Fourth Battalion under Commandant Ceannt. The Volunteers, with rifles and fixed bayonets, swung into College Green from O'Connell Street and formed a hollow square. I viewed the scene from the top of a tram-car at where King Billy's statue used to stand, and below me, on the street, I noticed, as an interested spectator, Viscount Powerscourt. I mention this because immediately after the Rising in 1916 Viscount Powerscourt was appointed Provost Marshal. After the inspection the various Battalions returned to their headquarters. The Fourth Battalion marched to Dolphins Barn where they formed up, were addressed by their Commandant, and sang 'The Soldier's Song' before being dismissed. That, I believe, was the last appearance of the Dublin Brigade on the streets of Dublin.

As the Irish in England were liable to be conscripted, many patriotic Irishmen left and came over to Ireland. Amongst those who came were Michael Collins, the two Nunans, Sean and Ernie, the four King brothers, and others. These men were housed at Larkfield, Kimmage, which was the Headquarters of the Fourth Battalion. They remained there until the Rising. Members of

Cumann na mBan were requested to obtain old tweed costumes to be converted into sleeping bags for the men. Friends also contributed such things as baskets of eggs and other articles to help in the catering.

When Eamonn Ceannt told me that the Rising was to be on Easter Sunday he told me that Thomas MacDonagh, who was a Commandant, had only been informed three weeks previously that the Rising was to take place, and that he seemed surprised but very enthusiastic. I cannot say if MacDonagh was a member of the Military Council for the three weeks prior to the Rising. I have no recollection of his being at a meeting of that body in my house, but they may have met elsewhere. About this period there was in circulation for about six weeks a very advanced paper, written all in Irish and entitled *An Barr Buadh*. Eamonn Ceannt contributed to nearly every copy of this, and I think Pearse was Editor. During the week before Holy Week there were several alarms in the city. On one occasion a ceilidhe was in progress and word came to the men that there was to be a raid for arms, I believe at the place where the arms were stored. The Volunteers immediately left the hall and stood on guard until the danger passed. I had hoped to go to this ceilidhe, but my husband refused to go as he did not wish to be at a social event when there was any likelihood of arms being seized by the police or military.

On Palm Sunday Eamonn returned from a meeting of the Volunteers, probably an Executive meeting, which had been held in the city. He told me that they had been discussing the posts which each of them should hold when the fight was over. 'Personally', he added, 'I was very pleased that I was chosen to be Minister for War.' I asked him, 'What of the others?' and although I think he said either MacDonagh or Pearse was to be Minister for Education I am not positive, as I really did not take the matter seriously. I remember he did not make any reference to a post for Eamonn de Valera, who was a Commandant, and I asked, 'What of de Valera?' He replied, 'Oh, he says he'll go down in the fight, whereas Tomás MacDonagh says that he will come through, as he always falls on his feet.' The other posts do not come to my memory in any way, not even the position at President.

I asked Eamonn how long the fighting would last, and he replied, 'If we last more than a month we will have won.' It must be understood that at this period I had no knowledge whatsoever of the date of the intended Rising, nor at any time did I visualise the Volunteers going out to attack. My idea was that they would defend.

That same night I had received an invitation from George Irvine, Captain of 'B' Company, Fourth Battalion, to a ceilidhe which was to be held on Low Sunday, 30th April. Having been denied an evening at one ceilidhe, I said to my husband, 'We'll go to that at any rate.' He looked at the card and merely said, 'Perhaps.'

About the middle of February, 1916, Liam Mellows had been arrested under D.O.R.A. He was placed in Arbour Hill barracks and ordered to be deported and to reside in England in a restricted area. The Volunteers were determined to get Liam Mellows back to Ireland, and I was deputed to see Mrs Mellows every other day on her return from Arbour Hill and report as to whether Liam was still in the country. It was arranged that he would reside with relatives in England, and immediately he left Ireland the Volunteers intended to act. About 14th or 15th April his brother, Barney, was sent over to visit Liam. When he reached the house where Liam was staying they both retired to Liam's bedroom and immediately a change of clothes was effected. In the clothes was a ticket for Ireland, with full instructions what to do. Liam reached Ireland safely, although the English friends were terrified when they learned of the substitution that had taken place. Barney decided he might as well go home too, and he arrived back in Ireland by a different route.

I was asked to prepare a bed for Liam, and this I did, but I was not called on for my hospitality, as Frank Fahy took Liam in to his house in Cunningham Road. The problem now was to keep Liam in hiding until he would be required.

On Monday of Holy Week Eamonn informed me that he was taking a week's holiday from his office as he did not wish to be caught like a rat in a trap. He suggested that I and our little son, Rónán, should accompany him to St. Enda's. (At the risk of repetition I include at this stage an extract, amended slightly, from an article written by me and published in *The Leader* of 20th April, 1946). Arrived at St Enda's, now closed for the holidays, we were admitted and sent out to the garden at the rear. It was a glorious morning, sun shining, birds singing, fruit trees in full blossom, and everything promising peace and plenty. In the distance, coming through a vista of trees, I noticed a young cleric approaching. He drew near, all smiles, and soon I was clasping the hand of Liam Mellows disguised as a priest. He shook hands with Rónán, and I said to the child, 'An aithnigheann tú é?' and he promptly replied, 'Althnighim.' Then Mrs Pearse and Pat joined us, and while the men chatted, she and I admired the green-houses, and the tree known as Sarah Curran's tree. Soon lunch was announced, and we went into the dining-room.

There were present at that meal: Mrs Pearse, her daughter, Maggie, her two sons, Pat and Willie, Liam Mellows, Eamonn, Rónán and myself. We had a pleasant lunch, the conversation roaming from books to music, but with no word of the impending fight. After lunch, Rónán and I were sent out to wait in the front grounds, and we bade goodbye to our hostess and hosts. I never saw the two Pearse men again. That wait in the grounds seemed an eternity, but at last Eamonn appeared and we started for home. It was then I got my instructions, and realised that the visit was in reality a business one. I was told that when it was dark I was to accompany Mrs Mellows to St Enda's so that she might bid farewell to Liam who, next day, was being moved to Galway. That night as we started out, I carried a basket ostensibly for eggs, which I occasionally bought at the lodge of the College, and to ensure we were not followed, we changed trams four or five times.

We arrived safely about 9.30. The house was in complete darkness and although we knocked, we could not gain admission. Louder and louder our knocking grew, until I feared the noise would bring every policeman in Rathfarnham around us. At length an upstairs window opened, and two small boys commenced to throw things at us. I recognised one small red-headed lad, and I asked him to tell Mrs Pearse I was at the door, but he only jeered. My patience was nearly exhausted, and so I said: 'I know you and unless you immediately get Mrs Pearse I'll get you the worst caning you ever got in your life.' He disappeared and soon footsteps approached, and we were admitted. Even then no light was shown, and while Mrs Mellows, advanced to a back room, I sat in the hall in inky darkness. The next time Liam and his mother met was on his return five years later (in 1921) from U.S.A.

On Tuesday, Eamonn asked me for directions to reach Mount Pleasant Square as he wished to get in touch with Seán Fitzgibbon who, I learned later, was being sent south to arrange the distribution of the guns expected to arrive on the 'Aud' from Germany. He travelled south next day. On his return from Rathmines, Eamonn told me of the Secret Document which, he stated, Alderman Tom Kelly would read at the meeting of the Corporation next day, thereby giving publicity to it. The genuineness of this document Eamonn never doubted.

That night as we were retiring, he unearthed his Mauser pistol and placed it beside his bed ready for use, remarking: 'We are living in stirring times.' The Volunteers had already been ordered to defend their guns with their lives, and so he was prepared. As I silently watched him, he said: 'If we live through this night we will have drawn first blood.' When I awoke next morning I thanked God that the night had passed peacefully.

Wednesday was an exceptionally wet day, Eamonn left home early, and I went into the city to buy stores for the knapsack in preparation for the coming manoeuvres. I remember as I went along College Green passing Mrs Sheehy Skeffington accompanied by her little son, Owen, who was tripping beside her all unaware of the tragedy which, within a week, would overtake him.

Thursday was a busy day in Volunteer circles. In the early afternoon an important meeting was held in Woodstown House, Dundrum, where John MacNeill lived in the same house as his brother, James. Eamonn told me that he had walked back from Dundrum with Thomas MacDonagh, who remarked: 'Bulmer Hobson is the evil genius of the Volunteers and if we could separate John MacNeill from his influence all would be well.'

It was evident that the leaders were endeavouring to induce John MacNeill to agree to the coming fight, and it had taken some persuasion. Another meeting of Volunteers was held in the city later, and then from about eight o'clock onwards several people called to our house and saw Eamonn. I learned later that these were couriers being sent down the country with instructions for the coming Rising.

Con Keating, the wireless operator, who was subsequently drowned in the River Laune, and another man had been to the house some days before, and received from Eamonn a lamp which was, to be used to signal to the 'Aud'. I believe they also travelled south on Thursday. They also got a ship's V/S (Visual Signalling) lamp, which they brought to Tralee. This latter lamp was in the care of the Volunteers, and was buried by them when the boat failed to get in. About the year 1918 this lamp was presented to me when I went down to Tralee to speak at a meeting. The Volunteers had resurrected it, painted it in the Republican colours, and put photographs of Roger Casement and Eamonn Ceannt on it beneath crossed flags. This lamp showed a green light. Unfortunately I retained the lamp in my house and it was stolen during a very bad raid by the Auxiliaries in December, 1920.

At breakfast on Good Friday morning, I drew Eamonn's attention to a report in the paper of the arrival of a collapsible boat off Kerry, and the arrest of a strange man. He made no comment, but during the three o'clock Devotions I saw a Volunteer enter the church and look around until he saw Eamonn, to whom he whispered something and then left. The evening was fine and we went for a walk in the Phoenix Park. We sat on a seat overlooking the river, our backs to the Magazine Fort, and I noticed that there was a continuous stream of lorries leaving the Magazine; evidently the Fort was being emptied of ammunition. Eamonn was rather silent: the only remark I remember him making was, 'You can almost over-organise things.'

On Saturday he decided we ought to go to Dalkey to visit a friend, whom he intended to ask for the loan of field glasses. On the way out on the top of the tram he whispered to me: 'The man who landed in Kerry was Roger Casement and the man who got away was Monteith. If they catch Monteith they'll hang him.' We stayed for lunch at Dalkey but nothing would persuade Eamonn to remain later than four o'clock. He said he had to be somewhere at a definite time and would be forced to take a taxi if we remained, so we returned to the city.

It was on that Saturday night, about six o'clock, that Eamonn told me the news. He said they would strike next day, and his headquarters would be the South Dublin Union. 'There are rumours of a secret session of the British Parliament', he added, 'and that means either peace with the Liberals in power or Conscription. We Volunteers, an armed body, could not let this opportunity pass without striking a blow while England is at war. We would be a disgrace to our generation, and so we strike tomorrow at six o'clock. I shall not sleep at home to-night in case of accidents, but will stay with John Doherty at James' Terrace.' After tea he wrote letters to his two brothers, to be delivered next day by the Volunteer Post service, and then went out to Confession. Eamonn had stated that he wished to get a flag of Orange, White and Green. My sister, Lily O'Brennan, purchased the material, bunting, at Burgh Quay, Dublin, and brought it to Mrs Mellows, who made the flag. Came Easter Saturday and the Easter Water, and the flag was brought in and sprinkled with Easter Water.

Late on Easter Saturday Mr Phil Cosgrave, who, I believe, was Battalion Quartermaster, was leaving our house, and my husband asked me to give him the flag. This I did, and my husband said to Mr Cosgrave, 'Be sure and turn out the green side.' I presume he meant that he did not wish Mr Cosgrave to be held up carrying a Republican flag. During the week a note came to me from my husband, in which he said, 'Rinne mé bratach na hÉireann inniu. Mé féin do rinneadh é.' I am not sure whether it was the flag we had made that was hoisted, or something else. I still have portions of the bunting and the needle which made the flag.

Eamonn left home for Doherty's about ten o'clock, and I then told my sister, Lily, the facts. I had asked Eamonn if the men knew the position, and he told me that the Volunteers, and certainly, his Battalion, had been warned repeatedly that, some day, they would go out not to return. 'In the present case', he said, 'we could not risk telling the men that the fight will be on tomorrow, as at the time of the Fenian Rising as soon as the men were told about it they thronged the churches for Confession, and the authorities, knowing a lot of the men suspected that something was going to happen and immediately took action.' I imagine that at the last moment the officers were told what positions they would occupy.

Lily O'Brennan, a member of the Central Branch, Cumann na mBan, had been mobilised to attend on Sunday, and she was ready.

My orders had been to take my mother and the child to the home of Mrs Cathal Brugha who had kindly placed rooms at my disposal, and where I had already sent clothes and food, Eamonn remarking: 'Our house will be in the line of fire.' I retired to bed about twelve o'clock, and at two o'clock I was awakened by a knocking at the hall door. I opened a window and looked out, and a voice in Irish asked for Eamonn. Hearing Irish, I was reassured, and came down to find Cathal Brugha. I told him where he would locate Eamonn, and without another word he went away. Within half an hour Eamonn returned with all his equipment, guns, ammunition, etc., which he had brought with him. I was astounded, but he merely remarked: 'MacNeill has ruined us – he has stopped the Rising.' Keyed up as I was for the fight, I started to make suggestions, but Eamonn replied: 'The countermanding order is already in the hands of the paper. I am off now to see if anything can be done.'

It was five a.m. when he returned home and said he had failed to contact anyone. His first call had been to [Dr Seamus] O'Kelly's but, in his excitement, Cathal had omitted to say at which O'Kelly's John MacNeill had held his meeting, so Eamonn drew a blank. He had next gone to Liberty Hall, where James Connolly was, but the armed guard refused to waken Connolly. The Citizen Army had been brought into barracks on Saturday night, and the men said they dare not disturb Connolly. Eamonn decided that if Connolly knew the position he would not be asleep if he thought there was work to be done, so he left. His next move had been to call at the Metropole Hotel, where Joe Plunkett was staying. No better luck met him here as Plunkett had left word he was not to be disturbed until 9 a.m., so Eamonn came home. I gave him some hot milk and he went up to his room. The Angelus was striking as he lay down, and he said: 'If I sleep now I would sleep on dynamite', and he slept. It was not for long, however. About seven o'clock, a courier arrived with a letter from Liberty Hall. I went quietly into a bedroom and as Eamonn was asleep I decided not to waken him, as I knew he would have serious decisions to make during the day. I placed the letter beside his bed where he would see it the moment he opened his eyes. Before eight o'clock Mrs Mellows called on her way to Mass, and I told her we were in great trouble and to pray hard. 8.30 saw Seamus Murphy (Captain

'A' Company, 4th Battalion) and he wanted to see the commandant. I inquired if the matter was important as the Commandant had been out most of the night. He replied it was important and so I wakened Eamonn. He was down within two minutes, the letter in his hand, and, having disposed of Seamus, asked how long the dispatch was in the house. When I told him over an hour he immediately took his bicycle, and without waiting for breakfast or even donning collar and tie, departed for Liberty Hall.

As the morning wore on, our house was besieged by the men of the 4th Battalion seeking an explanation of the countermanding order they had just read in the morning's paper. I could give them no information, merely saying the Commandant had been called out early, but suggesting they wait. Soon our drawing-room was uncomfortably filled and the bicycles were stacked four deep in the front garden. To pass the time they asked Captain Douglas ffrench Mullen, who was a fine pianist, to play for them, which he did – and amongst the airs he chose was 'The Dead March'.

It must have been one o'clock before Eamonn returned and met the men. He instructed them not to leave the city and if they left home even for a walk they were to state where they could be got at short notice. After dinner Eamonn suggested that we go as far as Howth. I remember him standing silently staring at the Pier where two years previously the famous gun-running had taken place. Home again and tea over, Eamonn said he wanted to use the front room. Having seen that the fire was burning brightly I left him for a while. Then I went in and asked if I could help him. He at once said 'Yes', and pushed towards me a bundle of Mobilisation Orders to fill up. I asked what I was to insert and he replied: 'Oh, I forgot to tell you we strike tomorrow – write in Emerald Square 11 o'clock.' My task completed, I was next sent to MacCarthy's house nearby, to ask for couriers. On my way I met a young woman, Mrs. Keegan, who was going to Evening Devotions. She clutched me and said: 'Oh, what does it mean – Ned got orders to stay near home and he wouldn't even come for a walk with us.' I replied: 'Pray hard, Millie, there is a lot of trouble.' I dared not tell her that her husband was being mobilised for the morrow. Next day, her husband, Eamonn Keegan, was shot through the lung while in action in the South Dublin

Union. He rallied from the wound and although he lived for years, he never really recovered.

Arrived at MacCarthy's, I saw Dan and gave my message. 'That will be all right', he answered, 'we are Standing To, so to speak, and having a bit of a sing-song, the men will be over at once.' I had scarcely reached home when the couriers arrived. Eamonn slept at home that night, remarking: 'I may thank John MacNeill that I can sleep in my own house – the cancelling of the manoeuvres will lead the British to believe that everything is all right.'

We discussed the effect of the countermanding order, and Eamonn said that the Volunteers would have agreed to majority rule, but that the order had been issued to the Press without their knowledge and, without their having been consulted, therefore they felt that they should go ahead with their plans. I understood from Eamonn that at first John MacNeill was tardy about agreeing to the Rising. He then agreed and orders were issued throughout the country. He was inclined to wobble again, but Thomas MacDonagh said to Eamonn, when coming back from the meeting in Dundrum on Thursday, 'I believe MacNeill will be all right if we can keep him away from' (Mrs Ceannt does not wish to disclose the name of this person.) He added, 'As soon as we start I feel certain that MacNeill will be with us.' Unfortunately the cancellation order followed on Saturday night, and the Council was forced to go ahead after their meeting in Liberty Hall on Easter Sunday.

In justification, possibly, of Eoin MacNeill's action it must be recorded that the messenger who had been sent down to superintend the distribution of the guns which were to arrive on the 'Aud' had returned hastily to Dublin, and reported to Mr MacNeill that the 'Aud' carrying the guns had been scuttled. MacNeill hurriedly called together some sympathisers with the Movement, but I would not put them down as prominent Volunteers. In his haste to prevent, as he thought, a failure, he omitted to call the strong men into consultation.

After the order cancelling the manoeuvres had actually been issued to the Press, as far as I know, Tomás MacDonagh was summoned to give his opinion on the matter. I was informed that when Mr MacNeill asked Commandant MacDonagh for his opinion, MacDonagh looked round the room and replied, 'I owe no counsel to these men', and left the house. He then sought Cathal Brugha, who lived in the neighbourhood, and I understand that Cathal interviewed MacNeill and was very angry with him. He, Cathal, then made his way to Eamonn's house and told him what had occurred. In his excitement he omitted to say which O'Kelly's house was the venue for the meeting.

Easter Monday morning saw us up early, and soon there was a constant stream of men to the house. I remember seeing Bertie (Barney) Mellows who, I afterwards, heard, was on the Magazine Fort attack. Eamonn had put on his uniform and did not wish to be seen from the street, so I acted as door-keeper. When the last man had gone Eamonn said he must have a taxi to take an urgent message to Rathfarnham. This was not easy to obtain as, being a bank holiday, all the shops were closed and in those times there were no public telephone booths. However, a local shopkeeper kindly allowed me to use his 'phone and the taxi came and delivered the message.

My mother had been to eight o'clock Mass, and on her return I told her she would have to leave home after breakfast and come with me and Rónán to another house, She flatly refused to move, making all kinds of excuses about her 'things' not being ready. I replied that her clothes had gone before her to the other house. I did not waste much time arguing, but let her enjoy her breakfast. Soon it was time for my sister, Lily, to leave, and as she had got no mobilisation order from her own (Central) Branch she decided to join up with the Inghini Branch, who were attached to the 4th Battalion and were forming up at Weaver Square. Bidding her goodbye and wishing her good luck, we saw her go off complete with haversack and bicycle. Time was now passing and Eamonn proceeded to collect his equipment. He had a lot to carry – a large bag full of ammunition, an overcoat and a bicycle. I helped him to put on his 'Sam Browne' belt and then adjusted his knapsack, which was exceptionally large and protruded out beyond his shoulders. While dressing I asked him how long he expected the fight to continue, and he replied: 'If we last a month they – the British – will come to terms. We have sent out messages throughout the country, but as the men have already received at least two other orders, it is hard to know what may happen. I have made sure of Galway, where the finest men in Ireland are. My message to

Mellows is "Dublin is now in action!"' 'However,' he added, 'we will put our trust in God'.

Turning to Rónán, who was watching us, he kissed him and said, 'Beannacht leat a Rónáin,' and the child replied, 'Beannacht leat a Dhaide.' 'Nach dtiubhraidh tú aire mhaith dod mháthairín?' he asked. 'Tiubhrad, a Dhaide', said Rónán, and so they parted for ever. I would have wished to go to Emerald Square to see the men march off, but Eamonn asked me not to and so I embraced him, bade him good speed and he went out. My next duty was to get my mother and the child away, and though still protesting, I induced her to put on her coat and come with me. Then taking our basket of food – a pretended picnic basket – and accompanied by my mother and little son, I crossed the threshold of that house, which would never mean home to me again, and closing the door I said farewell for ever to my ten years of happy married life.

As soon as possible after Eamonn left to join the Fourth Battalion I left my house in Dolphin Terrace and set out for Mrs Cathal Brugha's house. Mrs Brugha had kindly offered to house us during the fighting, as my home would be in the line of fire. I had forwarded my clothes and food beforehand. I was hurrying with my mother and Rónán and all we possessed in the way of food. All the money I had in the world was in my pocket, and I had two dresses on me. I decided that the quicker we could get across the bridge the better, so I made for Sally's Bridge, as it was then called, and over the canal, where we could see the soldiers at the back of Wellington Barracks. We turned then to the right, round by the Greenmount Oil works, and there we met four or five Volunteers dawdling along in uniform with full equipment. My impulse was to go over and say to them, 'Hurry, you'll be late', but I decided not to do so. I do not know whether they reached the point of mobilisation in time or not. I think Eamonn left home about a quarter or ten minutes to eleven to go to Emerald Square. The fight was to start at twelve o'clock. As far as I know Eamonn went into the South Dublin Union by the back gate, that is, the gate at Rialto.

As far as I can remember I took a tram to Kenilworth Road, and another tram to Rathmines, where I took a Dartry tram which left us at the terminus. I did not know then where I was, and had to ask where Fitzwilliam Terrace, my destination, was. It was only about one hundred yards away, but we took the tram that far.

We arrived safely at Mrs Brugha's house, and soon after our arrival Mrs Brugha's sister, Miss Kingston, came in. She had been across town getting treatment at a hospital. The first thing she said was, 'I heard the shots.' This brought home vividly to us the fact that the die was now cast. Miss Kingston and I decided to go out and buy some food in the shops in the vicinity, and we noticed that the trans had ceased to run. That would be about one o'clock. We met a man whom we had known as an assistant in a provision shop in Rathmines. This man, like his comrades, was a Volunteer. He was cycling as hard as he could away from the city, and when we stopped him the first words he said were, 'Davey's is blew up.' Davey's was a public-house at the corner of Richmond Street at Portobello Bridge. I said to the man, 'What do you mean blown up? Do you mean the glass windows are broken?' He told us that he was clearing out. Miss Kingston said, 'Will you not wait and give a hand to your comrades?' and he replied, 'Not likely. I'm getting away.' That was our first experience of the Volunteer who did not fight.

I stayed in Mrs Brugha's house for the week. On Monday evening we looked out the window and saw a Company of Boy Scouts coming down from the mountains, evidently they had been on a route march. Whether they were Baden Powell Scouts or Fianna I do not know, but I think they were Fianna. A couple of nights afterwards Mrs Brugha went out late for a walk. She was accompanied by her sister and a friend who was marooned in Dublin, and to whom Mrs Brugha gave shelter. They were not gone out very long when suddenly the doorbell rang, and whoever it was never took her finger off the bell until I opened the door, when the three of them practically fell into the hall. They said they had been challenged to halt, up the road, but instead of halting they had run. Mrs Brugha was expecting her baby at this time.

Early on Friday morning we were awakened by military raiding the premises. Naturally they were wondering at finding so many women in the house and no men, but Mrs Brugha said that her husband was a traveller and had been held up in the country. That evening Mrs Brugha's brother, Father Kingston, arrived and told us that Cathal had been wounded. He made light of the injuries, and Mrs Brugha, though anxious, was reassured.

Although we could see the fires burning in the city we noticed on Saturday that there was very little shooting, and we made our way as far as Rathmines. There we were told that there was a truce, but nothing more. On Sunday at Rathgar Church I met Mrs Con Murphy, who told me of the Proclamation that had been issued, and that my husband's name had been signed to it. That was the first I knew of the proclamation. All day Sunday we waited eagerly for news, and on Monday we tried to cross the bridge but without success. Mrs Brugha was anxious to see her husband. We met some priests in Rathmines on Monday. One of them, I think, was Father O'Mahony who told us that the men would be interned and that the leaders were to be tried by Field General Court-martial. This was rather a shock to me and the priest then tried to make light of it. He knew how deeply I was involved.

Thursday morning's paper brought the news of the execution of Pearse, MacDonagh and Clarke, and I believe in that same paper it said that it was stated in the House of Commons that a sentence of three years' penal servitude had been imposed on Eamonn and three others. I do not know who the other three were. When I read this I was delighted, but at the same time I thought it very hard that MacDonagh, who to my mind had not been so deeply involved until the last moment, should have suffered execution.

On Friday afternoon I piloted Mrs Brugha to the Union to see her husband. I did not speak to him as we did not wish to draw the attention of the other patients to him. I met Father Gerhardt there.

On my return journey I called at my own home in Dolphin Terrace only to find it a wreck, having been raided by the military. Our food had been spilt, that is to say tea and sugar were inches deep on the floor, our tinned foods had been taken out and evidently a bayonet run through each of them, and doors and windows were smashed, but these had been boarded up by the neighbours. The brass buttons which I had removed from Eamonn's uniform, to replace them by green, had been taken from the place I had left them. When the British came to raid my house the people next door were a mother and daughter, and when they saw the military jumping the railings separating the houses and pointing their guns at my house, the younger woman had a seizure and died immediately.

During this period I was labouring under the delusion that my husband had been sentenced to three years, but my sister-in-law, who lived in Drumcondra, traced me to Mrs Brugha's home and told me that I need not believe what I saw in the papers, that four more had been executed, Willie Pearse, Ned Daly, Michael O'Hanrahan and Joe Plunkett. She suggested that I come over with her and call down to the priests in Church Street, where the only reliable information could be obtained. She also told me that the military escort sent for Mrs MacDonagh had failed to reach her, so that Mrs MacDonagh had no final interview with her husband before his execution.

Louisa Hamilton Norway
Royal Hibernian Hotel,
Dawson Street, Dublin
Tuesday, April 15th.

D EAREST G., – I am afraid by this time you will have seen a good deal in the papers to cause you alarm, and as it is impossible to get a letter or telegram through, I will write you a detailed account of what we are going through and post it to you at the first opportunity.

To begin at the beginning, the Sinn Fein movement, which is now frankly revolutionary and which must not be confounded with Redmond's Nationalist Party, has been in existence for years, but has always been looked on as a small body of cranks who were thirsting for notoriety. Redmond's policy has always been to treat them with utter contempt, and the Government adopted his view. Since the outbreak of war this movement, encouraged no doubt by German intrigue and German money, has grown by leaps and bounds, and about eighteen months ago a large number broke away from Redmond's National Volunteers and formed a volunteer force which they called the Irish Volunteers. They are frankly and openly revolutionary, and when it became known some months ago that they were obtaining large quantities of arms and ammunition various persons did all they could to open the eyes of the authorities to the dangerous situation that was growing up. But as the explanation was always given that the force was for national defence only, the Government failed to take any steps to put down the movement.

During the past six months the body has grown enormously, as many as seven hundred recruits being enlisted on one night, and of course doing enormous harm to recruiting for the Army. On St Patrick's Day they held a large review of several battalions, armed, and the trams were all held up for about an hour in College Green. Up to the last moment there was hope that this would be stopped, but protests were like a voice crying in the wilderness. Another time they held a final dress rehearsal of what has actually taken place when they 'took' the Castle, St Stephen's Green, and various buildings. About a month ago one of their meetings in the country was broken up and the two leaders arrested and deported to England. A huge meeting of protest was held at the Mansion House, almost opposite this hotel, and attended by the Volunteers, all armed, who marched in procession. After the meeting they marched down Grafton Street, singing 'Die Wacht am Rhein' and revolutionary songs; a slight disturbance with the police took place and some shots were fired. People began to ask anxiously what next? but the Government looked on and smiled and H[amilton] tore his hair...

People are appalled at the utter unpreparedness of the Government. In the face of a huge body of trained and armed men, openly revolutionary, they had taken no precautions whatever for the defence of the city in the event of an outbreak. At the beginning of the war H. obtained a military guard, armed, for the G.P.O., and they have always been there. When the outbreak occurred yesterday the armed guard were there, but with no ammunition! The sergeant was wounded in two places and the rest overpowered.

All night the firing continued. Between 1 and 2 a.m. it was awful, and I lay and quaked. It was all in the direction of the Castle.

This morning we hear the military are pouring into the city, and are in the Shelbourne Hotel and Trinity College.

The rebels have barricaded Sackville Street, and it is expected to be very fierce fighting over the G.P.O. It is terrible!

All our valuables were stored in H.'s safe and cupboard when we gave up our house, and all our dear F[red].'s books, sword, and all his possessions, which we value more than anything else in the world. We would not trust them with the stored furniture.

Yesterday afternoon the mob broke all the windows in various streets and looted all the shops. The streets were strewn with clothes, boots, furniture, tram cushions, and everything you can imagine.

While I am writing now there is incessant firing in St Stephen's Green, and we fear there may be street fighting in this street.

In case you have forgotten, I will put a little plan here.

Tuesday, 5 p.m.

This morning martial law was proclaimed (I will try and get a copy of the proclamation) at 11.30 and the rebels given four hours to surrender.

A cruiser and two transports are said to have arrived at Kingstown, with troops from England. At 3.30 p.m., as there had been no surrender, the troops started to clear St Stephen's Green, and raked it with machine-guns from the top of the Shelbourne Hotel and the United Service Club. We hear there are many casualties. N [eville] has just come in, and says a big fire is raging in Sackville Street in the shops opposite the G.P.O., supposed to have been caused by the mob finding fireworks in a toy shop. The fire brigade arrived almost at once and could easily have overcome the fire, but the brigade was fired on by the Sinn Feiners, making it impossible for them to bring the engines into action, and they had to beat a retreat and leave the shops to burn themselves out. N. says the troops are clearing the houses of rebels behind Dame Street and the region of the Castle, and there is a lot of firing. It has turned to rain, which has cleared the streets of people.

A telegram has just come from the Admiralty stopping the mail boat from crossing. No boat has gone to-day, and we are absolutely cut off.

All the roads leading out of Dublin are in the hands of the rebels.

H. and N. have just come in, having seen Dr W[heeler]. (now Major W.), Surgeon to the Forces in Ireland. He told them that so far we had had about 500 casualties, two-thirds of them being civilians, shot in the streets.

The first thing Dr W. heard of the outbreak was a 'phone message telling him to go at once to the Shelbourne as a man had been shot.

He supposed it was a case of suicide, so jumped into his car and went off, fortunately in mufti. In Nassau Street his car was stopped and he was ordered to get out by rebels. He attempted to argue, and was told if he did not obey instantly he would be shot. Had he been in uniform he would have been shot at sight. As a civilian doctor they allowed him to go, and he took his bag and ran. He found three men shot in the Shelbourne, and a boy was shot as he reached the door.

Wednesday, April 26th, 9.30 a.m.

Last evening was quiet till we went to bed at 10.30, when almost immediately a furious machine-gun fire began. It seemed just at the back of the hotel, but was really at the top of Grafton Street and the street leading to Mercer's Hospital... While we were dressing a terrific bombardment with field guns began – the first we had heard – and gave me cold shivers. The sound seemed to come from the direction of the G.P.O., and we concluded they were bombarding it. It went on for a quarter of an hour – awful! big guns and machine-guns – and then ceased, but we hear they were bombarding Liberty Hall, the headquarters of Larkin and the strikers two years ago, and always a nest of sedition. It is now crammed with Sinn Feiners. The guns were on H.M.S. *Helga*, that came up the river and smashed it from within about three hundred yards. It made me feel quite sick...

Thursday, April 27th

Last night the mail boat left carrying passengers, and if it goes this evening Lord S. may be crossing, and he will take this to you.

Yesterday afternoon and evening there was terrible fighting. The rebels hold all the bridges over the canal, one on the tram line between this and Blackrock, another at the end of Baggot Street, and the other at Leeson Street. The fighting was terrible, but in the end we took the Leeson Street bridge, and I hope still hold it, as this opens a road to Ringstown. We failed to take the other two.

At the end of Lower Mount Street the rebels held the schools, and there was fierce fighting: our troops failed to surround the schools, and in the end, when they at last took them by a frontal attack with the loss of eighteen men and one officer, only one rebel was taken, the rest having escaped by the back.

Yesterday, to our great indignation, the public-houses were allowed to be open from 2 till 5, though every shop, bank, and public building was closed – just to inflame the mob, it could not have been on any other grounds; and yet at 8 p.m., after being on duty from 5 a.m., H. could not get a whiskey and soda, or even a glass of cider with his dinner, as it was out of hours. I was furious!

I must close this, as Lord S. has come in and says he expects to go to-night and will take this and H.'s report, so I will start a fresh letter to-morrow.

Don't worry overmuch about us. We quite expect to come out of this, but if we don't N. is yours.

Saturday, 29th, 10 a.m.

Last night was an agitating one. The sniper was very active, and after dinner several shots struck the annexe, one or two coming through the windows, and one broke the glass roof of the bridge. Mr B., who never loses his head, decided to get all the people out of the annexe, with staff (about forty people); and all we in the main building, whose rooms look out on the back, were forbidden to have lights in our rooms at all. There was such a strong feeling of uneasiness throughout the hotel, and always the danger of its being set on fire, that about 10 p.m. H. said we must be prepared at any moment to leave the hotel if necessary. So we went up to our room and in pitch darkness groped about and collected a few things (F.'s miniature and the presentation portrait of him, my despatch case with his letters, my fur coat, hat and boots), and we took them down to the sitting-room, which H. uses as an office, on the first floor. All the people in the hotel were collected in the lounge, which is very large and faces the street, and the whole of the back was in complete darkness. The firing quieted down, and about 11.30 we crept up to our room and lay down in our clothes. When dawn broke I got up and undressed and had two hours' sleep. All the rest of the guests spent the night in the lounge.

This morning we hear an officer has been to say that the shots fired into the hotel last night were fired by the military. People were constantly pulling up their blinds for a moment with the lights on to look at the city on fire, and the military have orders to fire on anything that resembles signalling without asking questions.

Reliable news has come in this morning that nothing remains of the G.P.O. but the four main walls and the great portico. It is absolutely burnt out. The fires last night were terrible, but we dared not look out. Eason's Library and all the shops and buildings between O'Connell Bridge and the G.P.O. on both sides of Sackville Street are gone.

It is difficult to think of the position without intense bitterness, though God knows it is the last thing one wishes for at such a time. In pandering to Sir E. Carson's fanaticism and allowing him to raise a body of 100,000 armed men for the sole purpose of rebellion and provisional government the Government tied their own hands and rendered it extremely difficult to stop the arming of another body of men, known to be disloyal, but whose avowed reason was the internal defence of Ireland! In Ulster the wind was sown, and, my God, we have reaped the whirl-wind!

We hear that many of our wounded are being sent to Belfast, as the hospitals here are crowded, and the food problem must soon become acute. Mr O'B. told me his ambulance picked up four wounded, three men and a woman, and took them to the nearest hospital. The woman was dying, so they stopped at a church and picked up a priest; arrived at the hospital the authorities said they could not possibly take them in as they had not enough food for those they had already taken, but when they saw the condition of the woman they took her in to die, and the others had to be taken elsewhere.

If the main walls of the G.P.O. remain standing it may be we shall find the safe in H.'s room still intact. It was built into the wall, and my jewel-case was in it, but all our silver, old engravings, and other valuables were stored in the great mahogany cupboards when we gave up our house in the autumn, as being the safest place in Dublin.

4 p.m.

Sir M[atthew] N[athan] has just rung up to say the rebels have surrendered unconditionally. We have no details, and the firing continues in various parts of the town. But if the leaders have surrendered it can only be a question of a few hours before peace is restored, and we can go forth and look on the wreck and desolation of this great city.

So ends, we hope, this appalling chapter in the history of Ireland – days of horror and slaughter comparable only to the Indian Mutiny. This seems a suitable place, dear G., to end this letter, and I hope to start a happier one to-morrow.

Yours,
L. N.

Samuel Guthrie (Superintendent of Telegraphs) to the Central Telegraph Office Controller, GPO Telegraph Office Amiens St Railway Station Dublin, 6 May 1916.

With reference to the seizure of the G.P.O. on Easter Monday the 24th. ult by the Sinn Féin Volunteers I beg to report as follows:-

At 12 noon a great many of the wires – including all the cross channel wires – became disconnected, apparently close up. At 12.10 pm. I was informed that the Sinn Féin Volunteers were taking possession of the Public Counter and after a short time I heard the breaking of glass in the lower storey. On looking out of a window in the Telephone Room I saw that the windows of the Public Office and other windows looking into Sackville Street were being smashed, the fragments of glass falling on to and covering the pavement, and several members of the Sinn Féin party stood round the public entrance with rifles and revolvers. I at once got Mr P. I. Kelly to phone the Headquarters of the Army Command, the Police Office in the Castle, and also to Marlboro' Barracks asking for assistance. At 12.30 pm I was informed by the Sergt. of the Guard that the Rebels were forcing the stairs leading from Henry Street to the Instrument Room and he asked me to obtain assistance for him. I explained to him what we had already done to obtain assistance. The guard consisted of a Sergeant and four men. The passage leading from the head of the stairs to the Instrument Room was then barricaded from the inside by filling it with chairs, wastepaper boxes etc. in order to delay the entry of attackers as much as possible, the guard of one Sergeant and four men standing inside the Instrument Room prepared to receive the rebels if they broke through the obstructions. Several volleys were fired by the rebels through the passage into the Instrument Room but entrance here had not been effected when a short time before 1 p.m. a party of the Rebels gained an entrance to the Instrument Room by the Southern Corridor after having passed through the Dining Room. As there was only one sentry on that corridor he was easily overpowered. When it was quite evident that an attack on the Instrument Room was intended through the Northern Corridor I instructed the Female operators at that end of the Instrument Room to clear away down to the Southern end, and as time progressed and matters became worse I told the Females to go into their Retiring Room and put on their outdoor apparel in case they would have to leave the building. Before the Rebels made their appearance at the Southern end of the room I was told that an officer of the besieging force wished to see me on the Southern landing to arrange for the withdrawal of the Staff. I sent word to him that I would not hold any parley with him as I did not recognise he had any right to be where he was. A few minutes later the officer – whom I now believe was The O'Rahilly – accompanied by a few supporters entered the Instrument Room each carrying a revolver and told all the officials in the Room to clear out at once at the same time questioning each one of them as to whether he carried arms. At this time all the Females had left the Instrument Room.

By 1 o'clock the last of the Staff had left the building and were in Princes Street. I stood in Sackville Street for a short time and then walked towards Abbey Street where I met Mr Doak of the Engineering Branch. After conversing with him for some time we proceeded to Amiens Street Rail Office to see if we could pick up London or other wires there. On arriving at the Amiens Street

Office I found that Mr Pemberton (Asst Supt) and a few operators were already there, and we were able to get London on two wires. At 2 p.m. (I) spoke to the Superintendent London on one of the wires and explained to him the state of affairs and asked him to advise all Irish offices with which he had communication and also the principal English centres. About 2.20 p.m. I thought it advisable to try and reach Mr Norway in order that he might be acquainted with the position of affairs, and accordingly I went to the Hibernian Hotel, Dawson Street but I was informed that Mr Norway was, it was thought, in the Castle.

As the Castle was at the time invested by the Rebels I returned to Amiens Street Office and explained to the London Superintendent what I had done and told him that Mr Norway could not be reached for the present. The Superintendent London then said he wanted a man to be sent to Newcastle Hut to make some wire changes in conjunction with Nevin (the Relay Station). As Westland Row and Harcourt Street Stations were both in the hands of the Rebels I instructed Mr Pemberton to try to get a motor car at Thompsons or some other garage and proceed to Newcastle, and I also instructed Mr Boyle, a Telegraphist, to accompany him in case it was necessary that an officer remain at Newcastle Hut. Mr Doak (Engineer) succeeded in raising the Military Adjutant on the Amiens Street Station Parcel Office telephone about 4.20 p.m. And informed him we had a wire to London working from Amiens Street Station if he wished to communicate with London. At 5.5 p.m. a cypher message was received by Special Messenger from Commandeth Dublin (Military Headquarters) to 'Troops London' and duly dispatched. This was the beginning of the Military Telegraph Service between London and Dublin in connection with the disturbances.

During the evening one of the two London wires was put through to the Irish Office in London. As no length was available between the Castle and Amiens Street Mr Doak proceeded to the Castle to try and arrange an extension but he returned at 8.30 p.m. having failed to get into the Castle. We therefore transmitted the work between the Irish Office London and the Irish Office Dublin Castle by means of a telephone wire through Crown Alley Exchange. The Telephone Exchange wires did not appear to have been interfered with by the Rebels. As the ordinary Telegraph Office premises at Amiens Street Railway Station occupied a very exposed position it was deemed advisable to seek other more safe and larger premises, and Mr Doak arranged with Mr Campion, the Engineer of the Great Northern Railway Company, the use of the Drawing Room, a large apartment about 50ft x 30ft and as this room already contained large broad benches used for dealing with maps & plans the change was most satisfactory as the benches suited admirably for the fixing of Telegraph apparatus. The wires were run into the new office on the evening of the 25th ult. by an emergency cable, and all was in readiness for work there on the morning of the 26th ult.

On Monday and Tuesday nights it was possible for me to return to my home at 9 p.m. and 7.30 p.m. respectively for rest. On the morning of the 27th (Wednesday) it was with difficulty I reached the office at 10 a.m. owing to street fighting in a portion of the district through which I had to pass; as the day progressed matters in this respect became worse with the result that both Mr Sweeney, Acting Evening Supt, and Mr Doyle, Assistant Superintendent, could not get into the city for duty in the evening. I accordingly remained on duty that night and as the whole City became involved in the disturbances all travelling through the street was practically suspended and remained so up to Sunday the 30th when a portion of the City reopened for foot traffic. I remained on duty until 12 noon on Monday the 1st inst. The Staff was practically shut up in the Amiens Street premises from Wednesday morning until the following Sunday and Monday.

At 1pm on the 25th ult. (Tuesday) two additional wires were provided, one for London and one for Liverpool and each was fitted with a transmitter for wheatstone working, and as a precautionary measure about 2.30 p.m. all the wires in the Amiens Street Testbox, other than those we were working, were disconnected by Mr Doak – a barricade of sandbags was subsequently erected in the ordinary Telegraph Office to protect the Testbox. On the same day a confidential service from the Secretary Telegraphs London to the Controller Dublin was received to stop all private and press telegrams passing between the United Kingdom and Ireland and to hold until further instructed. I replied that the Service had attention so far as Dublin only was concerned as we were at present isolated from other offices in Ireland.

The wires available on the 26th (Wednesday) ult. were as follows:-

One to Liverpool (BM BE wire) Wheatstone ' London (LV DN1 wire) Wheatstone " I. O. [Irish Office] London (DN GW 1. wire) Sounder ' Horse Guards London (DN MR 1. wire) Sounder ' London (LV CK to LKV then via NV) Sounder ' Belfast (DN BE 2 wire) Sounder. Three Telephone circuits to Crown Alley Exchange. These latter were taken on loan out of different Railway Offices on the premises.

On the morning of the 28th ult. the Horse Guards wire was extended to Headquarters Dublin (Parkgate Street) and we became right on a wire to Howth Summit (DN Howth 2). On the afternoon of the 29th ult. we got through to Dundalk Junction on the usual Railway wire, and as we were pressed to Belfast with Constabulary priority work a second outlet to Belfast was obtained at 7.50 p.m. on TS BE 5.

At 8.15 p.m. on the 29th ult. a second circuit from Horse Guards to Headquarters Dublin was asked for but there was no Dublin Headquarters length available at the time. A length was however subsequently provided which gave Horse Guards two circuits to Headquarters Dublin.

On the 30th ult., in reply to a query as regards the disposal of a message for Balbriggan, the Telephone Exchange reported that the Balbriggan and Belfast Trunks had been cut near Swords. The wires available on this date (30th) were as follows:-

One wire to Liverpool (BM-BE wire) Wheatstone ' London (LV1. extended) ' ' I. O. London (DN-GW 1) Sounder ' Belfast (DN) BE 2) ' Two wires to Horse Guards and H(DN-MR 1 & LV-CK & Nevin extension) Sounder One wire to Howth Summit (DN-HPV 2) Sounder ' Dundalk Junction (Usual rly. wire) Sounder Three Telephone circuits to Crown Alley Exchange.

The work dealt with from the 24th ult. to the present time was purely on Military and Constabulary Service, no public messages being accepted for transmission, and all work was disposed of by key and phone.

The Staff responded most willingly to the demands made on their service and endurance. I enclose a statement showing the names of the officers who voluntarily attended at the office from the 24th ult. to the 1st inst. The Constabulary messages were without exception lengthy and being principally in cypher were intricate to deal with.

I have pleasure in testifying to the able and courteous manner in which Messrs Doak and Dawson of the Engineering Branch fulfilled the onerous duties imposed on them in connection with the providing of the different circuits during the period under review.

Captain E. Gerrard, Rathfarnham, A.D.C. 5th Division British Forces in Ireland 1916–1921.[8]

I was educated at Clongowes College, and received a Commission in the Army. I was posted to the Royal yield Artillery. I was home on leave at Easter, 1916. I heard that there were disturbances in Dublin, I went to see what was happening. I was in civilian attire. I was in Harcourt Street when I heard an about: 'Stop the man with the pipe.' I hastily removed my pipe and managed to escape. I did not know what was going on. I saw the insurrection troops assembling at the top of Grafton Street and going into Stephen's Green. I was specially struck with their magnificent physique. They were huge men. I realised there was something serious on, and I went home and got my uniform in a bag. When going home I met Sir Frederick Shaw, Bushy Park, and he told me to go into Beggars Bush Barracks. I arrived there at about eight o'clock on Monday evening. There were no arms in Beggars Bush Barracks. Thinking over it now, the G.Rs. were there – but their rifles were not service type – and they had no ammunition. My estimate, looking back, was that in Beggars Bush Barracks for three days there were Sir Frederick Shaw, myself, one

---

[8] B.M.H., W.S. 348

or two ranker officers, four non-commissioned officers, and about ten men, three of whom were invalids. That was the garrison until the Sherwood Foresters arrived. I was the only officer there who had seen a shot fired of any sort, except Sir Frederick Shaw. He told me that he had been in arms against the Fenians when he was in the Life Guards in 1867 at the Battle of Tallaght. We had nothing to eat. There was not a scrap of food. That went on for two days. Sir Frederick Shaw's coachman drove in and out with some food for the officers. What happened to the troops I don't know. I don't think they were fed at all. There was nothing in Beggars Bush Barracks if only they had rushed it.

One of my sentries in Beggars Bush Barracks, about Tuesday evening, said to me, 'I beg your pardon, Sir, I have just shot two girls.' I said, 'what on earth did you do that for?' He said, 'I thought they were rebels'. I was told they were dressed in all classes of attire.' At a range of about two hundred yards I saw two girls – about twenty – lying dead.

On Wednesday morning after the Sherwoods arrived, Major Harris organised a continuous barrage of rifle fire against the windows of the houses in Northumberland Road. About three rifles were laid on each window and at a signal by whistle at least ten rounds from each rifle were directed at each window. Our men were in the windows of Beggars Bush Barracks. They had sandbags. I often thought there must have been a lot of people killed, but what could they do. They were being sniped at the time.

While we were sniping in Beggars Bush Barracks I saw a Sinn Féiner. By some accident, he put his head up over the railway line well and I saw him. I said, 'there's one fellow going to have it anyway'. I loaded the rifle and at a range of about 200 yards I fired. I saw the bullet hitting a stone within two inches of his head. I think this was on Wednesday morning. I was very glad afterwards that I had not hit him. I had never fired that particular rifle before. Of course, if he had seen me, he would have done the same. I saw R.A. Anderson shot. He was Fr. Finley's Second-in-command, in the Irish Agricultural Organisation Society. He was shot by shotgun cartridge slugs through a loophole in Beggars Bush Barracks. He was in the G.Rs. He was shot by Sinn Féiners. At about four o'clock on Wednesday afternoon some of the Sherwood Foresters arrived in Beggars Bush Barracks – twenty-five – as far as I remember, untrained, undersized products of the English slums. Sir Frederick Shaw said to me – we were being very badly sniped from the railway bridge, South Lotts Road – 'you take Q.M. Gamble and those men, climb up on the railway line and put them off'.

I said, 'very good, Sir'. We got over the side of the Barracks and through the houses on Shelbourne Road and up on to the railway by a ladder. I was over the wall fire, followed by Sergeant Gamble. Soon as I got over the wall, at a range of about 200 Yards, about eight Sinn Féiners advanced from the direction of the city to meet us. I saw them coming towards us, firing. There was what they call a fairly sharp fire fight, These men were standing up, not lying down. They came out of their trenches to meet us. They were very brave, I remember. They did not know how many of us there might be. The first casualty was Q.M. Gamble. He was shot dead, under the right eye. I was the next casualty. I don't know how many Sherwoods were killed. One of them was wounded on the approach to the railway. The young Sherwoods that I had with me had never fired a service rifle before. They were not even able to load them. We had to show them how to load them. One thing, from the Army point of view, I would like to mention is that the Sherwood Foresters had Mark VI ammunition. It was very old-fashioned stuff.

Thomas Leahy, Member 'E' Company, 2nd Battalion, Dublin Brigade. Irish Volunteers, 1914 Member of Irish Citizen Army.[9]

I was active in the Labour Movement from 1912 and learned, through it, the way the workers of Ireland were being treated. With wages and working conditions and long hours of employment forced on them by the employers, somewhere and somehow, if these were not changed or improved, revolt against some employers must come. I attended all meetings, lectures and talks by James Connolly, Jim Larkin, P.T. Daly and other Labour Leaders and well-known leaders in the republican movement. However, I soon got to know that there were some who were keen on the work for independence and anxious to help in every way the people at home during the labour struggles...

Oscar Traynor spared no time or interest to make the 2nd Battalion the smartest in the Dublin Brigade, which was confirmed afterwards by his appointment to O/C Dublin Brigade, by his system of attacks by Active Service Units both on the British forces and

---

[9] B.M.H., W.S., 660

Black and Tans; his method of raiding for arms and, where possible, the purchasing of same by each man out of his pocket money etc., which was encouraged by his own efforts. ...We were instructed to prepare for mobilisation orders for route march on Sunday, 23rd, together with the whole country taking their part, with members of the Citizen Army, Fianna Éireann and Cumann na mBan. Walking up Talbot St. on Saturday evening, 22nd April, after leaving Mrs. Holohan's shop in Amiens Street, where I usually called for papers and cigarettes, she seemed uneasy about something or other and advised me not to be from home for the weekend. I met my father and mother whom I had not seen for some time and whom I often visited. Father invited me to join him with mother and my family for the Easter Monday as he had heard that the mobilisation had been called oft for the Sunday by Eoin MacNeill. I was surprised, but made no remarks about it to my parents who then went home with my promise to meet them for a holiday outing to Phoenix Park on the Monday, which I kept, but not with them and under different circumstances which surprised them afterwards when they learned the reason. I got home that night feeling uneasy about the calling off order for to me it seemed a weakness of all our efforts. However after Mass on Sunday morning, I called at Mrs Holohan's, Amiens St. and there learned the truth about the calling off of the route march, etc. Her son, Hugh, called with another Volunteer named Sammy Reilly after dinner, when we discussed the countermanding of the mobilisation which we did not understand at the tine. We only hoped it would not kill the interest that was being taken in the Volunteers. After spending most of the day at my home, they agreed to come next day in case anything would turn up in the way of mobilisation or orders. They had not long to wait, for a knock came to the door about 10.30 p.m. When I opened it, it was Capt. Billy Byrne of 'E' Coy. of our Battalion the 2nd telling us to mobilise at Liberty Hall, Beresford Place at once and bring one day's rations for route march, when we would get further orders. The other two made for their homes at once for their rations and to inform their people of the route march etc. We met again at the placed named and found a fair crowd of Volunteers and Citizen Army men, Fianna Éireana and Cumann na mBan being served out with rifles, guns, ammunition, trench tools of all kinds. Captain Billy Byrne then called on men with cycles to stand out for certain orders; both of us did so. We were then handed some small arms and received orders to proceed with officer in charge, who would issue our orders when we arrived at the place to be attacked, which we discovered to be the Magazine Fort, Phoenix Park. The guard were to be disarmed, their arms taken, and tied up in the guardroom. Personnel were to be attacked, the keys of arms and ammunition stores taken; some of the arms and ammunition were to be destroyed, and as many of the arms as could be taken by us were to be collected by motor car which would be in attendance for same. After playing about with a football for some time to put the sentry then passing the top of the wall off his guard, we sat down in a group and each man got his instructions and, if successful, to report at the G.P.O., O'Connell St., which at the time we did not know was to be our headquarters.

We moved off in order, after saying a decade of the Rosary, and shook hands in case we should never meet again through capture or death. In the attempt some of the men were to ask that the gate be opened. They were then to take the guard by surprise and during this some others were to rush to the arms store, after taking the keys found on the guard. Those of us detailed to take the captured arms to the waiting car were to make our getaway the best way possible and report to the G.P.O. One man was shot dead on refusing to hand over the keys in the struggle for same. We got some rifles together with bayonets and got them safely in the car and made our getaway. I made for the Liffey gate on the Lucan road side and there found a crowd of people discussing the noise of the arms at the Fort exploding and wondering at the cause. I was stopped and asked had I been in the Park and what was the trouble. Of course, I acted as much surprised as they, just saying I had been cycling along from Lucan and stopped where I had seen them standing, hoping they might have been able to give me more news. Having a war service badge in my coat lapel, served to those on important war work while in Vicars Ltd, Barrow-in-Furness, they took me to be on holiday, and I passed on my way to the city. When approaching James's St. I ran into a large party of British troops emerging from a side street. All seemed to be very excited and were shouting to people to clear out of their way and keep out of the park. I just dismounted from the bike and went into a small paper shop and asked for some cigarettes till the troops passed on, for had I been stopped I had no doubts about what would have happened to me in the angry mood they wore in, as I was armed with two .45 Colt revolvers, and, having them in my possession, it may won have been my end. However, I continued on down Thomas St. and through High St. and around by the top of Dame St. I heard shots and firearms and sought cover by dismounting once again from the bike. It was the attack on the Castle by the Citizen Army men, who seemed to be doing well. I hesitate as to what action to take, being armed as I was. Not knowing the situation and having an order to report the Park attack, I decided to carry on. Coming out on the quay after passing out through the passage to SS. Michael and John's Chapel, I noticed a policeman on Capel St. bridge shouting to the people not to go towards Capel St. as the Citizen Army ruffians had captured the city and were in the G.P.O. shooting the people down in cold blood etc. He beckoned me to proceed down Aston Quay as it was the safest at the moment. I proceeded along that way to O'Connell Bridge. The people gathered there seemed to be hostile by their remarks and, fearing I might be delayed, and anxious to deliver my report, I continued down Burgh Quay across Butt Bridge passing Liberty Hall right on to Amiens St. to Mrs Holohan's shop. She was quite pleased to see me and informed me that the G.P.O. was now our H.Q. and to report there at once. Of course, I told her about our attack on the Magazine Fort and she was delighted.

The people about O'Connell St. when I reached it seemed dumbfounded and amazed and you could notice the change in most of them that at last the day had come when Irishmen and women were fighting for their freedom and the break from English rule. Many then and there went into the Post Office offering their service in any way of help or support. On arrival I was conducted to Comdt. James Connolly who, when told I had come from the Magazine Fort, at once informed P.H. Pearse, Tom Clarke and others. When I asked about my battalion and company I was informed they had taken up positions at Ballybough and Annesley Bridge, Fairview, where I had to report. On reaching same I was more than pleased to find Oscar Traynor, Sean Russell, Leo Henderson, Capt. Henderson, Billy McGinty, Pat Rossiter and his brother, Vincent Poole, Dan Courtney, Harry Boland, brother of Gerry, now Minister of Justice, John Redmond and others I forget their names; they were very busy erecting barricades on both bridges and taking advantage posts such as corner houses facing the railway lines, where it was expected that English troops from the north would be moving in on Dublin. Having got into work with the rest, Oscar Traynor gave orders when placing guards at the barricades, to allow no one through going citywards as many had already done who were not friendly to us or the movement, as we found out by their talk and attitude towards us afterwards. After the first day we had to lift rails from the lines opposite because it was learned that troops were on their way and this was to stop them and engage them. When the time came to do so, he organised a party of us to call at the homes of men who were mobilised but did not turn out to collect their arms, ammunition, etc., which were needed, as our supply was not too plentiful. After receiving their arms, we got orders from the G.P.O. to retire from our post at Ballybough and Annesley Bridges, as it was likely to be surrounded. During our stay there we captured some British officers returning from the city and who were dressed as policemen from the military camp, Dollymount. Harry Boland was given charge of them and, of course, they were taken with us to H.Q. After giving assurance to the shopkeeper who supplied the post with food and other goods we had requisitions in the name of the Republic, we packed up all our arms, material and food for the march to the city.

We had no information or news of the situation between the G.P.O. and our position and, at that time, the people were not over friendly to us judging by the remarks most of them passed. However, we met some who were friendly and helped us in many ways by clearing the street crossings and corners, together with handing parcels of cigarettes, food and other things to us as we passed. We did not know when we might come under fire from British troops who were then beginning to move towards the city. We reached Marlboro St. from the then Britain St. end, and we marched the whole length of same till we turned up a side street and heard heavy rifle fire taking place. Entering O'Connell St. we were fired on by our own men, then in Clery's and other large shops. One man named Billy McGinly was wounded but not seriously. After explanations were given firing stopped and we were given a right good welcome when they were told we were the Ballybough party. We then entered the G.P.O. after seeing the tricolour, our flag, flying over it, which gave us a thrill. Comdt. James Connolly, P.H. Pearse, Tom Clarke and other officers and men gave us a great welcome and congratulated us on the march from the last outpost. After a brief address we were then given orders to take over all shops and premises to the corner of Abbey St. from the Hotel Metropole. Entering the Metropole, we took some army officers prisoners who were staying there as guests home on leave from France. They handed over their arms and papers to our officer in command who, of course, told them they were prisoners of the Irish Republican Army now at war with England. They offered no trouble and stated they would give their word of honour to obey any orders given them, which they did, as we found out afterwards.

During this time the mobs from the back streess were busy smashing windows in the big shops and looting everything they could get their hands on. They were warned by P.H. Pearse that they would be fired on as they were bringing disgrace on the country and the Irish people. Of course, there were no police to stop them, they having been taken off the streets, so the mob were left to do as they liked until the firing started and bullets were flying all around the street.

Meantime, we were busy breaking our way through the buildings, erecting barricades and posting men at the windows and all advantage positions for defence, if attacked. Oscar Traynor, as far as I know and remember, gave the orders. The whole populace was very much dumbfounded and their long-suffering under the economic conditions and low wages for their labour made than more determined to grab all they could. It was a pity to see them, especially able-bodied men doing this kind of thing, instead of being in the firing line with us. We got as far down the street through the buildings till we stopped at the corner of Abbey St. at Manfield's boot shop, where strong barricades were erected as the windows were directly facing the buildings down Abbey St. which were being taken over by the troops. These buildings were: Messrs. Tucks, Engineers;

Dunlop's Rubber Showrooms; the Abbey Theatre; White's Delph Store and others. We discovered that snipers were on the roofs and getting the range of our positions. We came under heavy fire. Oscar Traynor, Vincent Poole, Sean Russell and myself kept replying to their fire which was continuous, till a lull in the evening, but afterwards kept up from Trinity College and during the next day, Wednesday, 26th April 1916. In this post were the men from the Ballybough area, namely as far as I can remember, Oscar Traynor, Sean Russell, Vincent Poole, Dan Courtney, Walter Carpenter and his brother, Joe Connolly, Robert Killteen, George King, myself and others. It was there I realised the coolness and tact of Traynor under fire. During the next day, Thursday, we observed through strong field glasses taken from the British officers in the Metropole many British troops on the roofs of those shops and buildings. Poole opened fire on them and some were seen to fail from the roofs to the ground. On the opposite side of the street our lads were doing well up to that time. When they were being surrounded a priest came out of the building and started to paint a Red Cross sign on the wall of a chemist's shop our forces were in. We marvelled at him, for the bullets were falling all around the place he was painting the sign. During that time Poole kept us all in good fettle by his tales of his experiences in the Boer War; his advice and caution were very useful as we found out when the sniping would start. He seemed to smell the different kinds of bullets and the direction they came from, and many snipers fell to his shooting during intervals and periods of rest.

The future was often discussed by us and what would be the outcome of it all; there were no regrets or complaints for what we had started. During one of the quiet periods Comdt. Connolly paid us a visit to see what all the firing at our post was for. After it had been explained to him about the snipers in Abbey St. and the D.B.O. lower down to the bridge, he warned us to be careful as that might be a ruse to keep us engaged while troops were creeping up or digging themselves in for a stronger attack on our position. This came true later that night. I was on guard while the other men were trying to snatch a brief sleep which was badly needed by all of us, for we had had little time to do so from the moment we took over this position, with breaking through walls, searching through the houses, erecting barricades and being on guard duty all that week, we were ready for a nap any time. I thought I saw a light appear at the window of the D.B.C. I waited before reporting to Traynor or Poole to see if it would appear again. It dawned on me by its nature that it was a cigarette being smoked, by its rising and falling. I took the risk to fire on it and all hands jumped to their post wondering was the great attack on, for the reply, to my fire was terrific. By it we found out that the British troops had crept into the building from the corner of Eden Quay and had also taken Hopkins and Hopkins, Jewellers' shop. We got it hot from then onwards and our men from that side of the street began to make dashes over to our side, for the buildings started to take fire and very soon the whole place was a huge inferno with maddened horses rushing about that had escaped from burning stables. We remained at our post as did the men in the buildings up to the G.P.O. Suddenly we got word from Oscar Traynor that we had to retire to the G.P.O. for instructions. When we arrived there we were paraded by the men in charge and afterwards addressed by P.H. Pearse, who thanked us all in the place for our stand and explained the reason for our recall. As the G.P.O. had been bombarded all day by artillery and was well on fire, we would have to leave it. The fire had taken a good hold on the buildings by that time and arrangements were then taking place for the evacuation. I remember, when chatting to a small group of men and women about the position, a burst of fire came on and a young Englishman, who was a friend of Seamus McGowan and a supporter of the Citizen Army, got hit in the stomach and died in a few minutes. We had to leave his body after us, but before we did so, a few prayers were said for the repose of his soul. I believe his name and address were found on him and his people informed in England afterwards. To me it brought back the memories of the men in Barrow-in-Furness.

However, orders were given to make for a lane opposite in Henry St. in batches, at short intervals, for a heavy machine-gun post was very much in action from somewhere about Jervis St. That was the first time we of the Manfield post had heard of the wounding of Comdt. Connolly, who had to be carried across the bullet-swept street together with the other wounded and all our arms and useful material to enable us to carry on. It was successfully carried out just before the roof fell in flames. On reaching the lane we found ourselves outside a mineral water factory which we entered, and this gave a welcome respite to all especially to the wounded. It was then discovered that we would have to turn into another lane to reach the houses in Moore St. No time was lost in deciding what to do. The O'Rahilly asked for men with bayonets to rush the barricade or machine-gun post held by the British troops covering the whole of the street. The idea was to cover our men who had to erect a barricade or obstruction for all in the mineral water factory to cross into the houses in Moore St. In the rush and charge I stumbled and fell due to having a heavy load on my shoulders. I found myself being helped to my feet by P.R. Pearse and Vincent Poole. Having got across the danger spot then under fire I found all my comrades of the post safe. At this stage, in looking round for entry to the houses, a Volunteer named Harry Coyle was killed by a sniper's bullet while trying to open the side door of a shop in the lane. He had come right through the whole week without any injury. However, I whispered a prayer in his ear and moved the body to one side.

An entry had been made by this time to the house and the wounded safely looked after, including Commandant Connolly. After a short discussion between the staff on the situation Oscar Traynor informed us that we had to get to the end of the Street through the walls of the house like we had done in O'Connell St. and, if possible, to link up with Comdt. Ned Daly in Britain St. who had taken Linenhall Military Barracks from the British. He then said to me 'You are a boilermaker or shipyard rivetter and used to heavy hammers and we must get through those houses, so you can get started, and myself, Poole, H. Boland will help all we can and cover you from any hostile people in the house you get through.' No one worked harder during that time there than H. Boland, Traynor, Poole, myself and others like Dan Courtney and George King. We got as far up the street as we could and that was to an ice cream saloon, when we got orders to stop. This was Saturday morning, 29th April 1916. The reason, we found out afterwards, was because the people leaving the houses we entered who, I must say at this stage, particularly the older were very pleased to know what was happening and were pleased they were alive to see the attack on England for freedom, and many blessed us and said prayers for our safety before they left their homes which, in many cases, were the last for these innocent people, some of whom were shot down in cold blood while advancing to the British lines with hands up as non-combatants. I remember P.H. Pearse coming into this room and seeing for himself what was taking place as regards the fate of those people. He instructed us to stop and have a rest till we got further orders. All of us were pleased at the order to rest and just threw ourselves on the floor from pure exhaustion. The next thing we heard on being wakened up was that there was a Truce or ceasefire on. We could hardly believe such a thing was possible after working so hard to strengthen our new positions. However, after hearing the situation explained to us by Sean McDermott (afterwards executed), he asked us to accept the order of surrender, particularly for the safety of the people in the area and the wish of our leaders. It was a bitter blow to us all at Moore St. We were so confident that at least the fight could have lasted a while longer to give time for the country at large to reach Dublin to carry on. We took those orders with a sore heart, especially from Sean who seemed very troubled, before finally forming up in the street from the houses we were in. A discussion took place amongst us about handing up our arms, for to most of us they meant many sacrifices as we had to pay for them from our pocket money from time to time both Volunteers and Citizen Army men. After a bitter argument about them, some decided to break them up, some to bury them in the yard of the shop we were in.

Maeve MacGarry,
Member of Cumann na mBan,
Dublin 1916.[10]

My mother was an active participant in the founding of Cumann na mBan. She brought me with her to the first meeting at Wynn's Hotel which founded Cumann na mBan. There was a good number of women present. Those I remember were Mrs Wyse Power, her daughter Máire, Mrs Kettle, Mrs Skeffington, Iza Lawler (Mrs Hughes now), I think Miss Bloxham, one of the Plunkett's (Philomena I think), Miss O'Rahilly...

Near one o'clock on Easter Sunday night there was a knock and Mother knew the meaning of it and said to herself as she went down the stairs, 'This is the call.' She opened the door and admitted Miss Marie Perolz and Charlie Wyse Power.

They came into the dining room and told her they had a despatch for her from Pearse. They gave her instructions about what she was to do next morning. She was to take the despatch to Limerick to Daly's house, where she was to contact [Michael] Colivet. If he questioned her she was to give the password ('Sarsfield').

She took an outside car to the station and went by train to Limerick. She was accompanied by Milo [MacGarry] who at the time was young and frail and she thought it best to take him out of the

---

10 B.M.H., W.S. 826

City. Also she felt if anything happened to prevent her from reaching her destination, Milo could get away more easily with the message. She was not at all nervous. On the contrary, she felt triumphant that she was the bearer of the message to her own town. I remember how exultant she was. It was the 9.15 train she took. As I saw them off at the door, after I had given them breakfast, I noticed the streets were extra lively. There were people gay going off to Harcourt Street station and to the Dalkey trams for the Easter Monday outings. A short time afterwards they were all trailing back, frustrated by the Volunteers who turned them back at the various points. Soon after my mother left, Miss Sorcha McMahon came in person to mobilise me. She had a list of Volunteers I was to mobilise first. Then I was to go into Jacobs. I told her that my mother had gone to Limerick and I was alone in the house with my father and the two maids, and that I had ammunition in the house. I asked her what I was to do with it. She told me that it was known where the ammunition was and somebody would come to collect it. I felt I could not leave until the ammunition was collected and, when I said this, she told me to do whatever I thought best. She then advised me to get some Volunteer to do the mobilisation if I could not manage it myself. She left and then I prayed earnestly that some Volunteer would come. Almost immediately Maurice Danaher, a friend of Milo's and a Volunteer in 'C' Company, 3rd Battalion, came. He is a barrister now, living in Rathgar. I gave him the list and told him to mobilise the Volunteers on it. After that Lilah Colbert came – a sister of Con's – and May McDonnell, who afterwards married Con's brother. He lost a leg in the Civil War. Several Volunteers then called to the door to ask where they were to go. As I had memorised the list, I was able to tell them. I had not seen them before but I remembered the names. Theobald Wolfe Tone Dillon, a brother of James Dillon, T.D,, came on the Tuesday. He afterwards became a priest. Three others who, like him, were not on the list came for instructions and I suggested they should go into the College of Surgeons. Maurice Danaher met them on Wednesday and they had not got in anywhere.

Maurice Danaher was in and out during Tuesday and Wednesday, bringing ammunition from various places. I don't know where he got it. One or two lads came in looking for ammunition and he gave it to them. During his various journeys, he collected quite a lot of information about how things were going. Another man who came was Denis McMahon. He was from Raheen in Clare and was manager of McLysaght's shop in Lower Baggot Street, at the corner of James Street where Conor Clune and his brother, also from Clare, were employed. It was called the Co-Operative Stores. In the whole of Fitzwilliam Street and Square there was nobody but enemies of our cause. These people described the Rising as a riot, adding that the police would soon put it down. When on Tuesday they found the gas cut off and all the shops shut, they had to admit the real position. There were two snipers on the neighbouring roofs. One seemed to be on the roof of the big house in Leeson Street facing Fitzwilliam Place; the other on the roof of a house in Lower Pembroke Street. He was very busy sniping during the whole week. I went out our back door to Lad Lane and saw the police in the Barracks collected at the windows, watching Plunkett's house and ours – I expect for snipers.

I went out on Monday for bread, also to explore the possibility of going into the College of Surgeons, although I knew I could not stay there on account of my responsibilities at home, as I have already described. I got as far as the Shelbourne Hotel that day and had to turn back. I met Eamon Curtis there and it was he who advised me to turn back, saying I could not get any further. At Merrion Row, at the entrance to Stephen's Green, I saw a dead horse. I was told it belonged to a cabman who insisted on going on his journey although told by the Volunteers to turn back. They shot his horse and must have taken away his cab, because it was not to be seen. On Wednesday morning about five o'clock I saw the British military arriving. They crept along on their hands and knees along the railings from Baggot Street into Upper Fitzwilliam Street where the residents gave them every help in their power, food and comfort of all sorts. Those were all people who were holding jobs under the Castle Government, although practically all of them were Irish and many of them Catholic. Some of them were the landlord crowd, others lawyers, judges, etc. There were very few doctors in the Square or Street then, except those who had also jobs under the Castle regime. I should have mentioned that on Monday afternoon I saw many of the wounded G.Rs being brought into the military nursing home next door to our house. I had seen a few of these G.R. men, whom I knew, in the neighbourhood who had set out in the morning dressed in their grand uniform on their route march, returning to their homes in the afternoon, looking very crestfallen.

During Wednesday morning Mrs Skeffington came in to see us and incidentally to collect ammunition. I gave her something to eat and then she went away carrying the ammunition in her umbrella and in a pocket which she had specially made inside the tail of her skirt. She came again in the afternoon and, by this time, we had heard from Maurice Danaher that her husband had been arrested. She had just been to the College of Surgeons – apparently she was in and out there – and she was in a very nervous condition although the average onlooker would not have noticed that. But I knew her so well and I could see she was terribly upset. She was so courageous that, even if she had any inkling of her husband's arrest, it would not stop her carrying out the task she had been given to do. Maurice looked at me to see whether he should tell her. I bowed my head and he informed her. She replied in a low tone, 'I surmised something had happened to him. I must get on with the work'. She had been asked at the College of Surgeons to secure a doctor. We wondered whom we would get and Maurice suggested Dr Michael Davitt; and he went down to Merrion Square for him. Dr Davitt came up with Maurice at once and Mrs Skeffington told him what he was wanted for. He consented to go to the Surgeon's but only on condition that he would not be kept – he probably had other patients. She gave him the password – 'Sarsfield' – and he went back, I think, to get his bag and then went to the Surgeon's. I held her for a while chatting. We went out into the garden to give her time to get over her shock. She went away then and I did not see her again that week.

From Wednesday the firing from the British machine guns became intense, especially in the neighbourhood of Mount Street. From our top floor windows we could see the military firing from the square tower of Haddington Road Church. It became very dangerous to move around in that area and the streets became quite deserted. A young priest came up from Westland Row Church warning the people not to go down there and not to go to Mass on Sunday. On the previous days they were to be seen going down in groups to the Church.

Of course, during these days we had no bread, no milk – except tinned milk which I had bought on the Monday – no meat. There were so many coming in and out that all our food was consumed. My mother had laid in a side of bacon but that was gone too. We never went to bed the whole week. The nights were terrifying.

On the Monday after the surrender our house was raided by a band of detectives accompanied by a military officer and a guard. They came in by the back; forcing in the back door. Lad Lane police barracks was right at the back of our house. They went through the whole house, asking questions about the inhabitants, especially about my mother. I told them she had gone to the country for the Easter holidays. I remained in the hall the whole time for fear Maurice Danaher, or any other Volunteer, might come. I wanted to warn them. I was not interfered with by the raiders. As it happened, Milo came to the door and I opened it and warned him to go away. My mother had come back earlier in the day from the house of some friends in Mountjoy Square (Miss Magee and her grandmother, Mrs. Lennox), where she had been obliged to spend the whole week after her return from Limerick. She had gone back to Mountjoy Square again to take some provisions to her friends as none could be obtained on the north side. The raiders did no damage and went away. They also raided Plunkett's house, No. 26, about the same time. They found nobody; the family must have been in Larkfield. My girl friends – all of them except Lilah Colbert – who had stayed in our house the whole week, went back to their own lodgings. Later in the week another raid was made by the military.

Milo MacGarry, Member of Irish Volunteers Dublin, 1916.[11]

On Easter Sunday, 1916, at about 4 p.m. Miss Perolz and Maebh Cavanagh arrived at 31 Fitzwilliam Street, and told us the Rising was to take place that night and we were to wait until we got a further message. The news of a Rising was a surprise. I asked was it Pearse and Connolly. They told me that there was a slight difficulty – a difference of opinion. They mentioned that Pearse, Connolly and McDermott were in it, and that there was a meeting in progress in Liberty Hall. They told me about Casement, that he had been arrested and was in Dublin, and would be rescued. I was satisfied when I heard these three were in it and that the girls had come from them. They told us that we were not to take any notice of any orders from anyone else. It was my mother they came to see. We were to do nothing until they came again; and they would bring a car when the final message was ready; the meeting was still in progress.

I was a member of the 3rd Battalion and I never expected anything of the kind, or suspected that a rising was at hand, though T. MacDonagh had given me a hint a short time before if I had been astute enough to take it in: 'We'll have Dublin to ourselves next

---

11 B.M.H., W.S. 356

Sunday, so don't forget.' All that day we waited indoors and, when midnight came, we decided that nothing would happen. I went out to see how the city was. I saw nothing, and came in and went to bed and to sleep. About two o'clock my mother was just going to bed when she heard a knock at the door. She opened it and saw Marie Perolz and Charlie Power, who had come from Sean MacDiarmada. They gave her a written sealed despatch which we understood contained the words: 'We strike at noon. Obey your orders.' It was addressed to Colivet and signed by Pearse. They told my mother to take the 9 a.m. train to Limerick, and deliver it at John Daly's house. She was to come back, if possible, and say whether she could deliver it.

I accompanied her to the station for the 9 a.m. train, by outside car. We went to Limerick. I am positive it was not the 6.45 a.m. train. At Ballybrophy, I saw Mary W. Power in the Cork part of the train. We arrived in Limerick shortly after 1 p.m. We went to Daly's. Madge was there and old John. They told us that the Volunteers were in Killonan. They took charge of the message; and two of the sisters took it to Colivet immediately. We were told that O'Rahilly had come the previous morning with the countermanding order and that, as a consequence, the Volunteers had been demobilised. The Daly's were debating what could be done, as the confusion was great. As it seemed likely that we might be in Limerick for some time, they gave us the address of a working-class boarding house in Hartshorn Street. We went there and booked our rooms, and came back, say, about 3 p.m. Seán Ó Muirthile had arrived in very bad humour. He said they were completely confused as a result of the different orders and he was very angry with Pearse. He told us that the Volunteers were in action in Dublin. He said: 'Whom am I to take orders from?' He went out, but he did not go back to the camp. We had a meal and then went to the station to see was there any news. We saw a notice chalked up – 'The usual 4 o'clock train running to-day.' We made up our minds that the Rising had collapsed. We decided we would go back to Dublin. We went back to Daly's where we found Edward Dore. The two Miss Daly's, Dore, my mother and myself made up our minds to travel to Dublin independently and as if we did not know each other. The Daly's meant to go to Tom Clarke, and Eamon Dore with them. We would try to contact Seán McDermott, or someone else.

We left the station in the train, but at Nenagh the train came to a full stop and we were all told to get out – 'This train is going no further.' An Englishman who was travelling said he would see the Company, as he would miss his boat connection. His voice was continuously heard above the commotion. We walked into the town and tried to get a car for Dublin. We had a long dispute with the railway official. There were many British military on the platform, returning from leave. The train returned to Limerick, and we all travelled in it. When we arrived back at Daly's, Mr McInerny, the driver of the car that fell into the Laune river at Ballykissane Pier, was there. He was on the run and did not wish to stay in his own house. Quite a number of other people were there, including Volunteers, one of whom was Seán Ó Muirthile, with whom I shared a bed that night. The house was put into a state of siege. Mrs Clarke's boys were there. Nothing happened.

There was no incident on Tuesday until 4 p.m., when the Dublin train ran again, and we all decided to travel by it – Ned Dore, Laura and Nora Daly, my mother and myself. We again agreed to act as strangers to each other. We reached Dublin very late; it might be near midnight. We did not know anything about events in Dublin till we got to the Curragh where we saw troops in war kit on the platform. At every station we came to, we thought we were going to be held up. When we arrived in Kingsbridge, the military were in possession. Before reaching Kingsbridge, it had been decided that the Daly's and Ned Dore would make their way to Tom Clarke's, round by Arbour Hill, Oxmantown Road and North Circular Road. The military shepherded us the same way, and we kept together till we reached Doyle's Corner.

My mother and I went to 11, Mountjoy Square where Diarmuid Lynch was staying – he was, of course, at this time in the G.P.O. – and there we remained parked until the following Monday morning. Owing to the cordon encircling the city, we could not get out, though on Saturday we got as far as Findlater's Church. Mrs Wyse-Power was also inside the cordon at Cole's, and Mrs Joe McGuinness was one of the first persons we saw. She was very active about Red Cross work. We saw William O'Brien who lived in Belvedere Place. He was arrested Sunday. We heard this after we came home. He told us he had left Connolly in Liberty Hall on the Sunday. According to him, Connolly had expressed the opinion that they were going out to the slaughter. A messenger, a girl, who had been in the College of Surgeons came through the cordon. She had been with Mrs. Connolly who, I think, was staying at the Countess Markievicz's cottage. She was a Citizen Army girl. When she had finished her story, she fell fast asleep on the chair.

On the Saturday or Sunday, on Mountjoy Square we met a man – a tramp – who had come through the cordon. He told us that the G.P.O. had been burnt out and abandoned, that there was no trace of any of the men and that he did not know where they had gone. That was our first information about the surrender; there had been countless rumours. It was after this we tried to get out via Gardiner Street, but a tommy with a cockney accent stopped us. 'It would be easier to get to Boston than Fitzwilliam Street', he said. The cordon was lifted on Monday. We passed along fairly easily. We were not allowed to have our hands in our pockets.

When we arrived back at 31 Fitzwilliam Street, Con Colbert's sister was there. She was lodging in Haddington Road, and came to our house to get news and could not get back. She was working in Lafayette's. She did not know where her brother was. Just as we had arrived and had got ourselves straightened out, I decided to escort Miss Colbert across Baggot Street Bridge. Then we got to the bridge, the cordon was still there and also at Leeson Street Bridge. They would not let us pass, so we had to come back to 31. I rang at the door, and it was opened slightly by a friend of mine, Maurice Danaher. He said: 'They are in.' We turned away and walked around the Square for half an hour or so, until we thought the raiders were gone. They were the military, accompanied by detectives, and had, cone in and gone out by the back. There was a full military raid on Wednesday when they also raided Plunkett's at No. 26. A brother-in-law (later) of Terence MacSwiney was among the raiders – Lieutenant Murphy. I was not there on that occasion either. They were looking for arms.

Richard Balfe,
Na Fianna and I.R.B. 1911–16,
Captain 'D' Company 1st
Battalion, I.V's.[12]

On the Good Friday previous to the Rising I was sent for. I proceeded to St Enda's College armed with small arms as instructed. We were used to escort a load of bombs from St Enda's to Church Street. On the Good Friday night we had all preparations in Blackhall Street and we expected to be going out on Sunday morning. We were 'standing to' all day Sunday and we got the mobilisation order on Monday morning at 10 o'clock that the manoeuvres were on. We were mobilised at George's Church, off Dorset Street. About twelve turned up out of about forty in the Company. Then we proceeded via Gardiner Street to Liberty Hall where the Company were left 'standing at ease' under the arches. I went into Liberty Hall with Heuston. It was about 11.15 or 11.20 a.m. when I arrived in Liberty Hall. When we entered we saw the Citizen Army 'standing to' under Sean Connolly. Then I was talking to Sean MacDermott and Mick Staines. They were all very business-like and slow-moving as they had been up all night. Madame Markievicz was going around with drinks; she was also moving slowly as she was

---

12 B.M.H., W.S. 251

tired like the others. I got my orders about 11.25 a.m. on a type-written paper without envelope. It was headed 'The Army of the Irish Republic'. I got orders to take the General Post Office in O'Connell Street, to enter by the side-door in Henry Street, to overcome all guards and to take possession of the building.

These orders were brought out to me from Sean Heuston and were signed by Connolly. I asked Heuston how I could manage with so small a Company and he said I would take all the Kimmage and Larkfield men. At twenty minutes to twelve I was called inside before Connolly, and I was asked did I know where the Mendicity Institution was and how long it would take me with my men to get there. He told me that the person who was assigned to take this place had failed. He was O.C. of 'G' Company, 1st Battalion. I was told to proceed there immediately, to take the building and hold it at all costs and to prevent all troops from passing to the city from the Royal Barracks. I was told to try to do this for two hours to enable the positions to be taken up in the City area. Although Sean Heuston had been appointed Commandant in charge of the G.P.O. and O'Connell Street area he elected to come with us. When we reached the Mendicity Institution we broke one small door and entered. As far as I recollect we found the place empty. We did not attempt to barricade it thoroughly as it would have been impossible, and we had not the material to do so. We occupied it. It was a two-storey stone building and in a recess from the main road (about 50 feet in). We occupied both storeys facing the Quays. On the stroke of 12 o'clock a small party of Sappers came along unarmed. We allowed these to pass knowing what was coming along. In a few minutes the main body of troops in-column on route came into view. We had sixteen men altogether including officers. All had Lee Enfield rifles. Every man had at least 100 rounds of ammunition. Myself and some others had 500 rounds each. Two shots were fired rapidly and the Commanding Officer dropped. I heard afterwards that he was shot between the eyes and in the heart.

The column halted right opposite to us after the two shots and it was a case of fire and one could not miss. The column were four-deep. There were from 200 to 250 at least in the column, At the time we had been putting out a Tri-colour Flag and we saw the officer in front drawing his sword and pointing towards it. This was the officer who was immediately shot dead. The firing became continuous and rapid and it eased off. Some of the British soldiers tried to protect themselves against the Quay wall and eventually ran up side streets and in through houses. The casualties were numerous and the ambulance was a considerable time removing the wounded. At 4 o'clock p.m. they came down eight-deep. They must not have known where the first attack had come from as the officer who first saw us was immediately shot dead. We altered our tactics then and we concentrated firing on the rear of the column. As they were nearly at Queen Street Bridge we suddenly concentrated the firing on the head of the column. The column stopped. It was just a matter of firing as rapidly as possible into a solid body. This column also broke up and ran in all directions. No man got past Queen Street Bridge. About this time we sent out a dispatch to the G.P.O. by two men, Paddy Stephenson and Sean McLoughlin, asking for information as to what we should do. The couriers returned next day and brought a message from Connolly congratulating us on the stand we were making and that everybody in the G.P.O. thought we would have been wiped out by that time. We received no message to evacuate.

On Monday night the British posted sentries right under us and shouted out 'One o'clock; Two o'clock, all well' and so on. These were withdrawn at daybreak. On Tuesday they took position in houses opposite to us and rifled the place with machine guns and machine grenades. They also took up position from Benburb Lane. On the Tuesday one of the famous British Bayonet Charges came down from the Royal Barracks with all regimental flags, fixed bayonets and swords. We used the same tactics as we had used on Monday concentrating on the rear first and then the head of the column. We believe that two of these men got across the bridge. The remainder went up Queen Street but returned as they were attacked by our troops from that end There was a lull for a time and it opened out then into individual sniping and the few that escaped took cover. They used machine guns on us but did very little damage.

On the Wednesday morning it opened up with machine-gun fire and we were completely surrounded. There was a laneway of escape. We sent out word by Stephenson and McLoughlin to know if we could retreat but no reply came back. Our ammunition and supplies were now exhausted. We came then under severe grenade and machine-gun fire. During this attack Willie Staines and myself were wounded by a bomb. Heuston bandaged Staines who was wounded in the head. I had lost complete use of my arms and legs but was fully conscious. Heuston ordered the surrender and put out a white sheet as a flag but we were immediately attacked again. Eventually the British accepted the Surrender but shot one of the men in the process, namely Peter Wilson of Swords. Being injured at this time I was left behind when the Company surrendered as I was thought to be dead. I am not familiar with what subsequently happened outside the Institute. Some time late in the evening I heard the British breaking in and then after an interval a British Officer appeared armed with two automatics; also a Dublin Fusilier arrived with, fixed bayonet. I was at this time able to sit up but had no use of my legs. While they were deciding whether to use a bayonet or a bullet on me an Officer of the R.A.M.C. came in and claimed me as his prisoner saying that there had been enough of this dirty work. I was removed to King George V. Hospital (now St. Bricins) where I received rough handling by Army Orderlies until rescued. Although not recovered I was removed in an armed ambulance to Richmond Barracks. I was removed afterwards to Wakefield and later to Frongoch. I was released at end of July 1916.

Every man in the Mendicity Garrison was tried by Military Court and sentenced to death. A great number of casualties had been inflicted on the British by them. As far as I remember the following constituted the Garrison of the Mendicity: - Sean Heuston, Richard Balfe, Liam Staines, Frank (John) Cullen, John J. Derrington, Liam Derrington, Thomas Kelly, James Brennan, Joe Byrne, Sean McLoughlin, Patrick J. Stephenson, Edward Roche, William O'Dea, Fred Brookes, J. Levins. On Tuesday evening we were reinforced by Dick Coleman, Joe Norton, John Clarke, – Meehan, – Peppard, – Marks, – Crinnigan, four men named Wilson, and two men named Kelly, all of the Swords Company.

Annie O'Brien and Lily Curran Cumann na mBan, Dublin, 1915–1924.[13]

I think it was on Thursday or Friday night at a meeting in 6 Harcourt St. that we got our instructions to mobilise on Sunday at that address at 5 o'clock in the afternoom. We all turned up at the appointed time in spite of the countermanding order which was published in the *Sunday Independent*. The attitude of the groups of Volunteers we knew was that they would take no notice of that sort of order. They were too anxious for the Rising and they were trained to obey the officers immediately over them and all these were keen to go out. We hung around 6 Harcourt St. for a while; finally our officers told us to go home and await further orders. Eileen Walsh (now Mrs Martin Murphy) and Rose McNamara were our officers. It was Rose who was in command of my section.

Marcella Cosgrove, who is now dead, was treasurer or quartermaster at that time when we returned home we had the same experience, as during the morning. The Volunteers were in and out moving ammunition etc. There were a number of Volunteers from Dunboyne and we had to provide meals for them and others. We had to stay at home that evening and night to take in any messages coming for Con Colbert who was away attending meetings and

[13] B.M.H., W.S. 805

who was expecting to get any minute, the mobilisation order for the Rising. This message would come from Eamonn Ceannt who was officer in command of the 4th Battalion. The first message – not, as far as I know, a mobilisation order – came about 10 p.m. by a courier, Tom Doran, who was a member of 'C' Coy. We passed this to Christy Byrne, who was next in command to Con Colbert. He dealt with it. No further message came until after Con's return. Some time around 2 or 3 a.m. Seoirse Irvine came with a message which Con dealt with himself. Some time about 7 Sean O'Brien, who was also a member of 'C' Coy, brought the actual mobilisation order, as far as I can remember. I offered to take it and keep it for Con who was then asleep. He would not give it to me but insisted on giving it himself to Con.

He went into the room, woke him up and gave him the dispatch. Con got up at once and then the hurry and bustle started. He got into his navy blue suit and went off on his bicycle to 8 o'clock Mass and Holy Communion. He told me to have his breakfast ready when he came back. I did so. He was not back for a while because he went to give a few mobilisation orders. When he came back he sent my brother, who was very young but a member of the Fianna, to Eamonn Ceannt to offer his services as dispatch carrier &c. While he was out he went to Mr Young's house – three of his sons were in F/Company – to mobilise them and send them with mobilisation orders to the company. My sister Lily was sent to Larry Murtagh to mobilise the Chapelizod section of F. Company. She went on her bicycle before we got our own mobilisation orders which came exactly at 9 o'clock. She got back in time and in the meantime we asked my other sister Eileen to go to our Cumann na mBan mobilisation point to make sure that they knew we were coming and to explain that we still had work to do for the Volunteers before going out to Weaver's Hall in Donore Avenue where our section was to mobilise. Lily, when she came back, and myself were feverishly busy filling Christy Byrne's and Con Colbert's haversacks and our own with any food we could find. They were both now in uniform. We helped them to buckle on the haversacks and Sam Browne belts and they were all excited to get out. During the time I was buckling him up Con – who had not a note in his head – was singing 'For Tone is coming back again'. He was so excited and charmed that at last the fight was coming off. He thought of nothing else.

The pair went off, wheeling their bicycles which were loaded up with pikes, their rifles and small arms. We saw them off at the door and waited till they were out of sight. Then we got ourselves packed up and were not very long after them. When we arrived at the Weaver's Hall most of the section were there – twenty-four or twenty-five of us in all. We had to wait there for the word to tell us where we were to go. While waiting we did a bit of Irish dancing and amused ourselves generally. Word came for us to march down to Donore Avenue. We halted head on Cork St. and fell in behind Seamus Murphy's Company (A), which was about to take over Marrowbone lane Distillery. Con Colbert and Christy had led their Company (F) to Watkins' Distillery in Ardee St. We marched into Marrowbone Lane Distillery after the Volunteers just as the Angelus was ringing. Rose McNamara led us in. We were taken off – one squad of us in which I was – to the front of the building and the rest to the rear of the building. We had a full view of the front gate and could see everything that was going on. When our rations were exhausted we had to provide food for ourselves and the Volunteers. Food that was passing by was commandeered and brought in. There was a butcher among the Volunteers who killed and prepared a beast that was brought in. This gave us food for a few days.

We were not long in the building when we heard the firing from the direction of the Union. Our captain was busy placing his men in position. I cannot remember whether our men had started any shooting that day. We had our quarters up in a barley loft and there was a sniping post just beside us, and the firing from there went on the whole week and our business was to look after the men who were there. There were other sniping posts in other parts of the building.

On Tuesday night a small band of C/Coy., who had vacated Roe's Distillery after their captain had left, joined our garrison. Among them were the three O'Brien brothers, Larry, Paddy and Denis (whom I afterwards married). I only knew their names at that time. They were brought up to our loft to rest. They had spent the night (Monday) trying to reach our post, having failed to get into the Union. We had been told that Con Colbert and his company were coming to join us as soon as they could and when I heard the footsteps on the stairs I thought it was they. I was quite disappointed when I saw the C/Coy. boys. They were all very young, most of them under eighteen.

At dawn on Wednesday morning the part of F/Coy. 4th Battalion under Colbert who had been in Watkins' Brewery arrived. They came in their stockinged feet to avoid detection by the British. The arrival of Con and his company put new spirit into the atmosphere of our post. Up to this the Volunteers' activity had been confined to the interior of the building; sniping from the different points had been kept up intermittently. One British soldier had been killed at the corner of Forbes Lane by one of our snipers who were posted on the bridge leading to the part of the distillery on the other side of the road. From the snipers' post at the back of the distillery there had been intermittent shooting towards the back of the Union and there was certainly one soldier killed there and possibly more. Immediately Con Colbert placed an outpost in an open position on the green sward near the bank of the canal. There was a public road between their position and the canal bank and they lay on the ground. From there they were able to pick off any British soldiers that attempted to enter the Union grounds from the back. The members of this outpost were changed from time to time and the place was regularly visited by Con. My late husband, who was an occasional member of this outpost and any of the others that I knew spoke highly of Con for having thought of this strategical plan. They admired him as a great soldier. That outpost remained active for the rest of the week until the surrender.

The members of Cumann na mBan had very little First Aid work to do. Nick Liston, who occupied a post at the back of the building commanding the back of the Union, was slightly wounded during the week. We bandaged his head and he went back to his post. He was very keen and a very good sniper. Our main activity was preparing food and generally looking after the welfare of the men.

My father visited us on Tuesday to see how we were getting on and to see if we wanted anything and to bring us a change of clothing. Someone had told him we were seen going into the Distillery. He came again on Wednesday. On that day he took messages from the

Inchicore men of the company to their people who were probably worrying about them. He was seen coming out of the Distillery by one of the 'Separation' women and she trailed him up along until he came as far as Kilmainham Police Station – he did not know this. She reported him to the police who arrested him and kept him in the station for the night. The next day the police handed him over to the military in Richmond Barracks. He was removed from there to Kilmainham Gaol where he was detained until he was deported to Wakefield with the other prisoners after the surrender. We three wondered why he did not visit us again and we only found out about his arrest on the Sunday of the surrender as we were forming up outside the gate of the distillery. Somebody shouted the information to us.

On the Sunday things seemed to have quietened down and the shooting had diminished. It was so quiet in comparison to the rest of the week that we decided to relax, and we were to have a ceilidhe that night. Seamus Murphy had given us permission for it if things continued to be all right. We had no Mass on Sunday. Earlier in the week we had a visit from Fr. Joseph A.U.B. one of the Mount Argus priests who heard all our confessions and gave us his blessing.

On Sunday afternoon a message came from Ceannt in the Union to Seamus Murphy telling him to be ready to surrender. The news was received very badly and there was great disappointment. There was dreadful grousing; they were saying 'Was this what we were preparing for and living for all this time? Is this the end of all our hopes?' They were flinging their rifles around in temper and disgust. Then word went round the whole distillery that we were to assemble in front of the building for the surrender. There were a few who refused to surrender and they cleared off. It took some time to gather them from all points of the building and to persuade them to obey the order. It was finally brought home to most of them that as soldiers it was their duty to obey the order of their leader.

While we were trying to get some of the last of them down I was standing at the window of the barley loft and saw the gate being opened by Sergeant O'Neill who had been in charge of it all the week – it was barricaded on the inside. When it opened who walked in but Eamonn Ceannt who had come down from the Union. He was like a wild man; his tunic was open, his hair was standing on end and he looked awful. He evidently hated the task of asking the garrison to surrender. He put his two hands on the barricade, with his head bent, and presented a miserable appearance. With Ceannt was a British military officer to whom he had already surrendered. There was a third person, but I can't now recall exactly who it was.

Then the garrison surrendered through Seamus Murphy and prepared to leave.

John Joseph Scollan,
Commandant Hibernian Rifles,
Dublin City Area 1916.[14]

I came from Derry to Dublin in 1911. Prior to this the A.O.H. American Alliance had held a conference in Dundalk and I came to Dublin as National Director…

On Easter Sunday the Hibernian Rifles paraded as usual in North Frederick Street. I had seen the Sunday paper which contained McNeill's cancellation order. We carried out our usual routine training on that date. Apart from MacNeill's orders to us Irish Volunteers I had a feeling that there was something serious afoot and I therefore ordered our units to again parade on Easter

Monday. At 12 a.m. on Easter Monday I was at the hall in Frederick Street and had about sixty men there. When the information came that the Volunteers had seized the G.P.O. the men were anxious to know what they should do. I addressed them and told them that as far I knew this fight which was just starting was unofficial, but as it had started we should join in and take our place in it. At the same time I said that if any man did not wish to volunteer for the fight he was at liberty to go home.

About thirty men elected to join in the fight. This party were all armed. I sent word to Connolly that I was ready with assistance when

---

[14] B.M.H., W.S. 318

he required it and asking for orders. He sent me a message which said he was very glad to get mine and instructed me to stay where I was and await orders. We secured supplies of food by commandeering from the local shops. At 4 p.m., I again sent a message to Connolly asking him to give us something to do as my men were getting uneasy. I suggested I should occupy Leavy's Public Rouse at the junction of Upper Dorset Street and Blessington Street. Connolly again sent me a message to stay where I was. At 12 p.m. that night I got orders from Connolly to proceed to the G. P. O. with my party. When I got there the first orders I got were to break and barricade all the upper windows. The O'Rahilly instructed me to do this. I also saw Connolly there. When we were finished. with the barricading of the windows we got some rest. At 6 a.m. on Tuesday I received orders to get over to the Exchange Hotel in Parliament Street. We proceeded the Metal or Halfpenny Bridge – eighteen of my men and nine Maynooth men. Incidentally the toll man was still on duty on the Bridge and tried to collect the halfpenny toll from us. Needless to say he did not get it. No attempt was ever made to collect tolls on the bridge again. En route we passed the Telephone Exchange and I never could understand why it was not taken as it only had a small guard of British soldiers. The British afterwards paid tribute to the assistance this was to them in quashing the Rebellion. We proceeded through the west end of Fleet Street and Cranes Lane. We went on to Shortalls beside the Exchange Hotel and there we found two men using the telephone.

These men had been in touch with the Curragh Camp. Sean Milroy took up the telephone and by listening got good information regarding the movements of the British troops which was conveyed to Headquarters at the G.P.O. by Milroy. We got into the Exchange Hotel and on to the roof. At this time some of the Volunteers were supposed to be trapped in the *Evening Mail* Office and in the City Hall. We found that the City Hall was occupied by British soldiers and we engaged them by fire. In the afternoon units of the Irish Fusiliers and Enniskilling Fusiliers advanced to storm our position and were met by a fusilade from our shot-gun men and Rifles. They were actually slaughtered by our fire. Twenty-three or four of them were killed or seriously wounded. I was on the roof near a chimney when a bullet caught Edward Walsh, one of our men, and literally tore his stomach out. He died that evening. Some time in the year 1924, 1925, 1926 or 1927 I contributed an article to the *Sunday Independent* giving an account of this engagement. This was a much more detailed account as my memory was much fresher then.

At about 4.30 p.m. that evening we received orders to retire to the G.P.O. The remarkable thing about this was the sudden change in the conduct of the inhabitants of the locality towards us. When proceeding from the G.P.O. to the Exchange Hotel the people were hostile towards us – now they were sympathatic and helped us to get back. On the way back to the G.P.O. two of our men were taken prisoner; they must have got detached from the main body and wandered into the British outposts around Dame Street.

Molly Reynolds, Cumann na mBan, Dublin First Aid Duty in Dublin, Easter Week 1916.[15]

After the Volunteers were formed they rented premises at 2 Dawson Street and Bulmer Hobson went there. We moved from 12 D'Olier Street to No.1 College Street. I am not sure of the date we left D'Olier Street, but I know we were in College Street at the time of the Howth gun-running because we took up the floorboards and put some rifles under the floor. My father was appointed Auditor to the Volunteers and in that connection T.F.O'Rahilly was a frequent visitor to our office. He was of a cheerful disposition and you could always tell when he was coming because he sang on his way up the stairs. On Thursday of Holy Week, 1916, he came to the office but this time he did not sing on his way up and when I asked him why he just replied: 'Ah, I am very sad to-day.'

We were mobilised for a route march on Easter Sunday and were told to prepare first-aid outfits in connection therewith. Some members of the Fairview Branch, as we were commonly called, met at our house and we proceeded to make the outfits which consisted of a small bottle of iodine, a bandage and a safety pin or two.

---

15 B.M.H., W.S. 195.

Early on Easter Sunday morning we got our mobilisation order and then we got the paper and saw that the orders were cancelled. One brother was in the Fianna, two other brothers and father were in the Volunteers and I was in Cumann na mBan. None of us knew what to do, so went to our different Headquarters for instructions and were told to stand-to. On Easter Sunday night I went to Liberty Hall to see if I could get any information. I met two of James Connolly's daughters, whom I knew, and they told me that they were going to Belfast that night I got no other information...

After a little time Margaret Skinnider arrived at the Green and said there were no women at the G.P.O. and she had been sent to look for volunteers for that post. The other member of Cumann na mBan and myself volunteered.

We met the O'Rahilly outside the G.P.O. and he welcomed us. He took us over the building to select the most suitable place for a first-aid casualty station. We eventually decided on a big open space at the back of the main hall. I do not know what it would have been used for as there was nothing in it except a huge table, unless it had been cleared of its rendered to him. Another serious wounding was James Connolly. He got a bullet wound in the left leg which shattered, I would roughly estimate from one and a half to two inches of his shin bone. There is a laneway running from Prince's Street to Middle Abbey Street, and Connolly left the Post Office to visit some outposts in Abbey Street, using this laneway to reach them. After he had been gone a short time we heard a shout for a stretcher. Another girl and myself picked up a stretcher but were not allowed to go out. We handed it to some men and they brought Connolly in. His leg was dressed, set in splints and a waste paper basket was cut in two to make a cage for it. A bed was procured and Connolly was placed on it. He refused to remain a patient in the Casualty Station and his bed was moved to the main hall where the headquarters were. The rest of the casualties were only minor ones.

The late Fr. Flanagan, who was then attached to the Pro-Cathedral at Marlborough Street, was with us most of that week. After the first day or two things more or less settled down and we were getting used to the sound of the guns. My father was in the Post Office and on Thursday morning he told me that the top portion of the building was on fire, that the men had it under control, but there was danger that the British would cut off the water supply. That night the barrage was terrific, it was bad any night, but that Thursday night is beyond description. It was the night the *Helga* shelled us from the Liffey. On Friday morning most of the girls working in the kitchen and acting as despatch carriers were sent out under a Red Cross flag. They were to go to their homes, but were arrested and brought to the Broadstone for questioning. Friday evening it was apparently decided that it was time to leave the Post Office, because we got instructions to move the wounded to Jervis Street Hospital. During the week the Volunteers had been making a way through the buildings, down Henry Street by breaking holes in the walls. They got as far as Arnott's. In some places the holes were near the floor, in others they were a couple of feet high. Through these holes the Red Cross men and women, wounded, excepting Connolly, and prisoners, accompanied by Fr. Flanagan moved off. We got as far as the Coliseum in Henry Street which was a place of entertainment. We halted here while some of the Red Cross men went forward to open an exit door which would let us out into Prince's Street. Here we were confronted with a barricade some feet in height at the opening of the laneway leading into Middle Abbey Street. We crossed the barricade and got into Middle Abbey Street, crossed over and walked down the opposite side of the street to where a public house just out at the corner of Liffey Street. Here we waited while Fr. Flanagan, the British Medical Officer and British soldiers went forward to make arrangements for the reception of the wounded at the Hospital. Fr. Flanagan, accompanied by a British officer in charge of a number of British soldiers, came back and we were escorted down to the Hospital. Here the British military arrested the Red Cross men and men with the minor wounds. The Hospital authorities took charge of the seriously wounded cases and allowed us to use a waiting room to the dispensary…We remained at the Hospital, all Friday night and portion of Saturday. Towards Saturday evening Fr. Flanagan came in and told us the fight was over, the men had surrendered and that we could go home…Most of us lived in the same direction and we had got a certificate from Fr. Flanagan saying we were in Jervis St. Hospital at his invitation and that the officer did not look at it but directed her on to our house.

Frank Gaskin,
I.R.B. Liverpool 1911/Irish
Volunteers, Dublin.[16]

I joined the I.R.B. in 1911 when I was in Liverpool. Pat Lively and Dan McCarthy, Liverpool, approached me. Pat Lively swore me in. I joined the circle in Liverpool. Pat Lively was Centre. The circle had no particular name. We met nearly every Sunday in the Gaelic League Hall in Bootle...

When the Volunteers started I joined up at the first meeting in the Rotunda... I took part in the Howth and Kilcoole Gun-Runnings as a member of 'D' Company, 4th Battalion. Cathal Brugha was the first O.C. of this Company. Ffrench Mullen became O.C. prior to 1916. I kept contact with Liverpool and succeeded in getting a supply of small arms which were brought by Ted Kavanagh who was a seaman on one of Tedcastle's boats. The Centres' Board used to meet in 41, Parnell Square once a month, on, I think, the last Thursday of the month. I recollect the following Centres of Circles; Frank Lawless, P.J. Farrell, George Lyons, Seán Murphy, Greg Murphy, George Irvine, Val Jackson, S. O'Connor, Seán Tobin, Peadar Kearney, Seán Farrelly, Luke Kennedy, Tom Hunter, Con Colbert, B. Hobson.

I was present at a meeting of the Centres' Board in 41 Parnell Square on Holy Thursday night. B. Hobson presided. At the meeting

---

[16] B.M.H., W.S. 386

someone said something about the Supreme Council having decided on a Rising on Easter Sunday. Hobson said that the time was not opportune. This was the first definite information I received that a Rising was to take place. I am nearly sure it was Holy Thursday as I recollect meeting on the following day, Good Friday, Dan McCarthy and Joe McGrath, and discussing the matter with them and deciding to go to confession in Mount Argus. We all did so on Holy Saturday.

I do not recollect being at any meeting of the Centres' Board on Good Friday or having got a summons to attend one. I did not parade on Easter Sunday as I got word that the Rising was off, I paraded on Easter Monday with my Company at Emerald Square. Garry Holohan came along and asked for four Volunteers. I volunteered along with Paddy McGrath and two others. We went to Rutland Street, off Summerhill, from there to the Magazine Fort with Paddy Daly in charge, Paddy Boland and I went and disarmed the sentry and held up the guard. We disarmed the guard. The remainder of our party tried to get into the explosives store but did not succeed. They set fire to some of the building. After about twenty minutes we left and I went to Marrowbone Lane to Seumas Murphy.

On Wednesday I got a message from Seumas Murphy to take to the Union but could not get in, also I took a message to Mrs. Cosgrave from Phil Cosgrave who resided opposite the Union. I then went to Roe's Distillery but found the Volunteers had evacuated it. I then went to the residence of Jack Mills in Mount Brown where I learned my brother-in-law, Charlie Quinn was lying badly wounded. He sent me to his home in Dolphin's Barn where I got a rifle and some ammunition. I was cut off by the military in the house and I used the rifle from the house. I was there until Friday. I heard of the surrender and I went home. On the following Monday I was arrested, taken to Kilmainham station and brought to Richmond Barracks. I was later transferred to Wakefield Prison. I was released from Wakefield in July. I learned later that Supt. McFeely of the D.M.P. who lived near me, sent in a favourable report about me.

An Onlooker's Tale.
The Story of the Irish Rebellion, by St John G. Ervine

On Easter Sunday, after an absence of several weeks, I returned to Dublin from England, and in the evening I walked down to the Abbey Theatre to obtain my letters. There was an air of festival in the town, for the rigours of Lent were at an end, and the people were making ready for such merriment as is possible in time of war to those whose men are in very present danger in Flanders and France; and as I crossed O'Connell Bridge and stood for a moment or two to look at the high reaches of the golden sky which are everywhere visible in Dublin it seemed to me that the 'peace . . . which passeth all understanding' had settled on this old, distracted city. There had, indeed, been murmurs and mutterings and marches of drilled men, and now and then one met an anxious official, full of foreboding, who spoke desperately of danger; but these were disregarded. One had stood on the pavement to watch the volunteers go by, and had treated them lightly. How could that tattered collection of youths and boys and hungry-looking labourers ever hope to stand against the British army!

One saw them, on St Patrick's day, marching up Westmoreland Street to College Green, some of them dressed in a green uniform that, except in colour, was a replica of the khaki uniform of the British soldier. Most of them had no uniform, and their cheap, ready-made clothes had an extraordinarily unwarlike look that was made almost ridiculous by the bandoleers and the long, obsolete bayonets and the heavy, out-of-date rifles they carried. The mind, remembering tales of France and Flanders and the Dardanelles, of guns that fired shells a ton in weight for many miles, of an extraordinary complicity of invention whereby men may be slain by men who have never seen them – the mind, remembering these things, found something supremely comical in the spectacle of young clerks and middle-aged labourers steeling their hearts and fitting their bodies with the worn-out implements of war in the hope that they might so disturb the British race that all they desired would instantly be conceded to them…

All day the rebels had been in possession of the city. The Government seemed to have thrown up the sponge. There was not a policeman to be seen, or a soldier or any person in authority. At ten o'clock that morning there had been a Government and policemen and soldiers; at eleven o'clock all these had disappeared. There was looting in O'Connell Street, some of it extraordinarily ludicrous. There was one looter who had stolen a dress-suit from a shop near O'Connell Bridge. He went into an abandoned tram-car stripped his rags off, and then put on the dress-suit. When he reappeared, swaggering up and down the street, he was wearing brown boots, a dress suit, a Panama hat, and he was carrying a lady's sunshade. The rebels tried to prevent looting. I saw them making the attempts, but their attempts were ineffectual, and all that day (Monday) and all Tuesday the looting went on ridiculously.

Although the Government had mysteriously vanished, and there were no policemen to arrest the looters, one did not feel that victory was with the rebels, nor did they themselves think that victory was with them. That anxious, waiting look had marked the rebels' faces all day, and now something of dread came to the larking crowd; and as the night fell, the jokes ceased, the laughter died out, and silence came. At seven o'clock the streets were nearly empty. I looked out of my window and saw shadow-shapes moving swiftly homeward, huddling close to the houses. The rebel sentries still guarded the gate of the green which faced toward Merrion Street, and through the gloaming I could detect the figures of boys and women hurrying about their business in the camp. A cab came down the east side of the green, and the sentries challenged the driver; but he would not stop, thought they called 'Halt!' a dozen times. Then they fired on him. The horse went down instantly, and the driver, abandoning it, leaped from the box of his cab and flew down Merrion Street. The poor beast, sprawled on its haunches, tried to struggle to its feet, but fell back as often as it rose. While it lay there, struggling and kicking, a motor-car came down the side of the green, and the driver of it, too, was challenged, and he, also, refused to halt, and again the sentries fired. I was leaning out of the window to see what happened, and I laughed, for the man who was in the car yelled out the moment he was hit:

'Oh, I'm dead! I'm dead!'

The car stopped suddenly, grating harshly on the roadway, so that one's blood curdled for a few seconds. Then the wounded man was taken out. The sentries gathered round him. 'Why didn't you stop when you were told?' they said reproachfully, and added, 'Take him to Vincents', the hospital a little way up the street. While they were supporting toward the hospital, the man went on moaning: 'Oh, I'm dead! I'm dead!' It was the worst imitation of death I had ever witnessed. They did not take him to Vincents'. They changed their minds, and took him into the green and treated him there. His wound was obviously slight; he could not have yelled so lustily or walked so well as he did if it had been serious. There was no dignity in him, only foolish bravado that speedily turned to squealing; and so one laughed at him.

After that there was a queer silence in the green. In the distance one heard the occasional rifle-firing, but here there was this ominous quietness. It became difficult to see, and so I closed the shutters; but before I did so, I looked toward the wounded horse. It was lying in the middle of the street not making any movement. 'Thank God, it's dead!' I said to myself, and then drew the shutters to.

There was a dreadful feeling of strain in the house, and I moved about restlessly. I got out the manuscript of a play on which I am working and began to revise it, but I could not continue it long. I tried to read a book by H. G. Wells, called *An Englishman Looks at the*

World. I had opened it at the chapter entitled 'The Common Sense of Warfare,' but I found that the war outside proved conclusively that there is no common sense in warfare, so I put the book down and tried to play a game of patience. I played three games and then I went to bed.

I slept in small dozes that were more exhausting than if I had not slept at all. The desultory rifle-fire had increased during the night, and it seemed to me that shooting was proceeding from the Shelbourne Hotel. At four o'clock I got up and looked out of the window. I was sleeping in the front of the house, and I had left the shutters of my bedroom open. It was not quite light enough for me, who have poor sight, to distinguish things clearly, but I could see a huddled heap lying in front of the gate where the sentries had been a few hours before. And the horse was not dead. While I looked, it made a feeble struggle to rise, and then fell back again. 'Why don't they kill it?' I said to myself, and I went back to bed. But I did not sleep. There were people moving about in the next room, fidgeting and fidgeting. I got up and began to dress, and while I was doing so I heard the sound of heavy boots on the pavement below, echoing oddly in that silence; and then I heard shots, followed by a low moan.

One's mind works in a queer way in moments of unusual happenings. I knew that someone had been shot in the street outside my home, and if I had been asked before the thing happened what I was likely to do, I think I should have never guessed correctly. I stood there counting the dying man's moans. He said, 'Oh!' four times, and then he died. I went to the window and looked out. It was now about six o'clock, and I could see plainly. The huddled heap outside the gates of the green was the body of a dead Sinn Féiner. The horse in the roadway was now quite still. Just off the pavement, in front of the door of my home, lay the body of an old man, a labourer, evidently, who had been stumping to his work. I suppose he had not realised the rebellion was a serious one, and had started off on the usual routine of his life; and then Death had caught him suddenly and stretched him in the road in a strangely easy attitude.

I came down-stairs, and the maids gave me breakfast, apologising because there was no milk. It seemed to them that one could not drink tea without milk. These minds of ours are amazing instruments. Outside the door lay the body of an old man, a little farther off, wearing a fawn-coloured overcoat, lay the body of a dead Sinn Féiner; at the corner of the street a horse had died in pain; and we were wondering about milk. Had the milkman funked?

I think it was between eight and nine o'clock that the ambulance came and took away the two dead men. The horse was dragged, I do not know how, to the pavement, and it lay there, offensive to the eye and nostril, for a week. People came to one and said, 'Have you seen the dead horse?' In whatever way conversation began, always it seemed to end with that question, 'Have you seen the dead horse?'

I remember now standing with a friend on the stairs, so that my eyes were on a level with the fanlight over the hall-door, and looking into the bushes just inside the green railings. I could see a young Sinn Féiner, rifle in hand, crawling on the ground; and then the soldiers at the Shelbourne saw him and let a volley at him, and he rose and ran, and we saw him no more.

Later on people came out of their houses and began to walk about. No one was allowed to cross the road to look into the green, and it was impossible to say whether any Sinn Féiners remained in it. The foliage obscured the view. There were rumours that many of the Sinn Féiners had been killed in the night, and that those who had remained had fled from the green and taken refuge with their comrades in the College of Surgeons; but there was no confirmation of these rumours, and it is doubtful whether they were true.

Toward ten o'clock the street filled. A few soldiers had been smuggled by back ways into the Shelbourne Hotel, and these commanded St Stephen's Green. Other soldiers, few in number, were stationed in various parts of the city; but to all intents and purposes Dublin was as completely in the hands of the rebels on Easter Tuesday as it was on Easter Monday.

I went down to O'Connell Street and found that during the night the Sinn Féiners had been busy. Each of the streets running at right angles to O'Connell Street was barricaded, in most instances ineffectively. Barbed wire was stretched across O'Connell Street in such a way as to form a barrier on each side of the general post-office. And on Tuesday, as on Monday, one saw the pale, 'rattled,' and very tired looking young rebels preparing for attack. On the other side of the barbed wire, beyond the Nelson pillar, were some dead horses that had been killed while being ridden by soldiers. One heard rumours of desperate fighting in other parts of Dublin. Some of the veterans' corps, who had been drilling in the mountains on Monday, had been shot dead by Sinn Féiners when they returned home in the evening. The lord lieutenant, the rumour ran, had been taken prisoner, and was now immured in Liberty Hall. The wildest talk was being uttered. It was said that the pope had committed suicide on hearing of the rebellion. It was said that Archbishop Walsh, the Catholic Archbishop of Dublin, had killed himself. It was said that the Orangemen were marching on Dublin in support of the Sinn Féiners.

It was on Easter Tuesday that the worst looting took place. Men and women and children surged up from the foulest slums in Europe and rifled the shops, stripping them almost bare. Some harsh things have been said about the looting, perhaps no harsher than ought to have been said, but I doubt whether in similar circumstances in any city in the world there would have been so little looting as there was in Dublin on those two days. One tries to imagine what London would have been like if it had suddenly been abandoned for two days to the mercy of the mob. I think a Whitechapel mob would have sacked it in that time.

While I was standing in O'Connell Street, Francis Sheehy Skeffington came up to me. He had half a dozen walking sticks under his arm, and he said to me: 'I'm trying to form a special constabulary to prevent looting. You'll do for one,' and he offered a walking-stick to me. I looked at the stick and I looked at the looters, and I said, 'No.' It was characteristic of 'Skeffy,' as he was called in Dublin, that he should behave like that. The pacifist in him would not permit him to use force to restrain the looters, though one might have thought the logician in him would have regarded the walking-stick as a weapon; but the hero in him compelled him, for the honour of his country, to do something to restrain them. On the previous day he had harangued them from the top of a tram-car, reminding them that they were Irish, and bidding them not to loot for the sake of Ireland's honour; and they had stopped looting – until he had gone away. To-day his proposal to overawe them with walking-sticks.

Here indeed, I could not but think, was Don Quixote charging the windmills yet another time!

I imagine that he was unsuccessful in his efforts, for later on in the afternoon I saw him pasting slips of paper onto the walls of O'Connell Bridge. The slips bore an appeal to men and women of all parties to attend the offices of the Irish Suffrage Society in Westmoreland Street and enrol themselves as special constables to maintain order. I never saw Francis Sheehy Skeffington again. That evening he was taken by a lunatic officer and shot in Portobello Barracks.

By this time the soldiers in Dublin had been reinforced, and troops were already hurrying from England. All that evening, as far as I could see, there was no stir in the green, but the firing was heavier than on the previous day, and all over the city there was the persistent banging of bullets. The windows on the ground floor of the Shelbourne were full of bullet-holes, and the wall of the Alexandra Club on the west side of the green was covered with the marks of bullets. That afternoon I had seen a dead Sinn Féiner lying inside the gate of the green that looks down Grafton Street, lying face downward in a hole in the earth, and I wondered whether he was the man I had seen the day before, intently watching, while the girls chaffed him. And while I was peering through the railings at the dead man, someone came up and said to all of us who were there: 'Poor chap! Let's get him out and bury him!' There were three women from the slums standing by, and one of them, when she heard what he said, rushed at him and beat him with her fists and swore at him horribly.

'No, you'll not get him out,' she yelled. 'Let him lie there and rot, like the poor soldiers!'

That speech was typical of the general attitude of the Dublin people toward the Sinn Féiners. Popular feeling was dead against them. Here was a singular rebellion, indeed! Men had risen against a power which they could not possibly beat on behalf of people who did not wish for their championship! Wherever I went in Dublin in the first days of the rebellion I heard the strongest expressions of hatred for the Sinn Féin movement. There was a feeling of remarkable fury against the Countess Markievicz, remarkable because this lady had spent herself in feeding and succouring poor people during the 1911 strike, and one would have imagined that some feeling of gratitude would have saved her from the insults that were uttered against her. A strange, incalculable woman, born of an old Irish family, she had thrown herself into all kinds of forlorn hopes. It was said that her most ardent desire was to be the Joan of Arc of Ireland, that she might die for her country.

On Easter Tuesday night, about ten o'clock, the soldiers on the top floor of the Shelbourne began to use machine-guns, and the fire from them went on, I think, for an hour. Up to then we had heard only the sound of rifles, and it was a very unimpressive sound. If this was war, we thought to ourselves, then war is an uncommonly dull business. We became bored by bullets. When the surprise of the rebellion was over, most of us became irritable. We could not get about our ordinary affairs, we could not take our customary pleasures, and the rebellion itself had become flat.

But the rattle of machine-guns made us all sit up. The marrow in our spines seemed to be crawling about in search of a hiding place. I do not know what to compare the sound that a discharging machine-gun makes. Some said to me that it resembles the sound of a lawnmower which has been turned upside down; but to me it sounded like the noise made by a stick which is drawn rapidly along railings. One sat there, frankly afraid, and imagined a perpetual flow of bullets pouring across the green, killing and wounding and terrifying. One wondered, too, whether the wooden shutters were stout enough to keep out ricocheting bullets. The sensible thing to do, of course, was to keep to the back of the house, or, at all events, as far from the front windows as possible; but one does not do the sensible thing in such times. Instinctively, one rushed to the window to look out when a shot was fired, as instinctively as the crowds in London, despite official warnings, rush into the streets to look at the Zeppelins. The overmastering desire to see what was happening will draw the most craven to the scene of disaster, and that accounts, no doubt, for the fact that people went every day to 'see the fighting' in Dublin, and could not be persuaded to keep indoors until the rebellion had been suppressed.

That night, that Easter Tuesday night, was, I think, the worst of all the nights. It was the first time we had heard the noise of machine-guns, and it was the only night that a lengthy spell of fighting took place in this part of the city. If rebels remained inside the green, their terror must have been akin to madness. I wondered vaguely what had happened to the three girls who I had seen busy there on Monday. I suppose they had been sent away on Monday, but if they had endured that rake of fire – I cannot remember now on what day the great fire of Dublin began. I think it was on Thursday. There were rumours that the Helga had come up the Liffey and had shelled Liberty Hall and I was told that the Abbey Theatre was lying in ruins; but it was impossible to get near O'Connell Street or obtain any reliable information as to what had happened. There were soldiers on the roof of Trinity College, commanding the general post-office and also the rebel strongholds in Dame Street, and the fire from their rifles and machine-guns made the approach to O'Connell Bridge a no-man's-land. One went down to the firing-line every day, and repeated all the rumours that one had heard on the way.

And then the fire began. I stood at the window of my bedroom and looked at the sky that was scarlet with flame. The whole of O'Connell Street and many of the contiguous streets were like a furnace, roaring and rattling as roofs fell in a whirlpool of sparks the splashed high in the air. The finest street in Europe was consumed in a night.

All this was in the centre of the city. In outlying places fierce fighting continued, and many men on both sides were killed and wounded; but of these things I knew nothing beyond what I subsequently read in the newspapers. I was bound inside the city, just beyond the zone of flames, and here there was little firing left. I could still see the republican flag floating over the College of Surgeons, but those who were inside the college were keeping very still. Now and then the soldiers in the Shelbourne fired spasmodically, and we could hear the sound of heavier and more regular firing further off; but for us, there was chiefly the flames flowing skyward from O'Connell Street. Almost one was glad that the looters had secured some stuff that would otherwise have been fuel in that terrible fire. No one can tell what caused the fire. Some say that it was started by looters, either intentionally or accidentally, and some say it was caused by the explosion of shells or ammunition. It is, I think, more likely that a careless looter began it.

In a few days Dublin became a city of nurses and doctors and ambulances. Wherever one went, one saw them with Red Cross badges on their sleeves, hurrying continually. Motor-cars, with large Red Cross flags flying at their sides, rushed about the town, laden with nurses and doctors and medical students, and every now and then an ambulance came swiftly to a hospital door, and some wounded man or woman or child was carried from it.

On the Saturday following the beginning of the rebellion, I walked out of Dublin to see a friend, and when I was returning in the evening I heard that some of the rebels had surrendered. A man came along the road, riding a bicycle furiously, and as he passed he leaned forward a little and shouted, 'They've surrendered!' and then went on. We had been heavy in our minds till then. The rebellion was getting on our nerves, and we were pessimistic about the future of Ireland. News had come to us, too, that a friend, a man of unique value to Ireland, had narrowly escaped death by accidental shooting. He had miraculously escaped all injury, but the shock of his danger hurt our spirits. And then came the news of the surrender, and suddenly the heaviness lifted. We doubted the truth of the news, but even in that state of dubiety there was relief. It seemed to us that the air became clearer, and there was a noticeable look of recovered happiness everywhere. When we came to the outer suburbs of the city we saw groups of people standing at corners, talking animatedly. 'it must be true,' we said, and hurried to join one of the groups; but as we hurried we heard the dull noise of rifles being fired, and the joy went out of us, and our pace slackened.

But the news was true. Some of the rebels had surrendered. Thomas MacDonagh and P. H. Pearse, finding themselves in an impossible plight, decided to surrender, and thus prevent the loss of more lives. A friend of mine, a member of the viceregal court, who witnessed the surrender told me afterward that Thomas MacDonagh came to the surrendering-place as coolly as if he were going for a stroll on a summer evening. P. H. Pearse was rather 'rattled,' and his head rolled from side to side, He was, perhaps, a more emotional man than Thomas MacDonagh, and he was frightfully tired.

I never saw P. H. Pearse, but I met Thomas MacDonagh once. He was interested in the Independent Theatre of Ireland, and one evening I went to see the tiny theatre in Hardwicke Street to see some performances he and his friends were giving there. I had only lately come to Dublin, and I knew none of the people connected with the Independent Theatre. A friend introduced me to Thomas MacDonagh. I remember him chiefly as a man who smiled very pleasantly. There was a look of great gentleness about him. He sat beside my friend for a while, and I was so placed that I saw his face easily.

He was a man of middle height and slender build. His high, broad brow was covered with heavy, rough, tufty hair that was brushed cleanly from his forehead and cut tidily about the neck, so that he did not look unkempt. His long, straight nose was as large as the nose of a successful entrepreneur, but it was not bulbous, nor were the nostrils wide and distended, as are the nostrils of many business men. It was a delicately shaped and pointed nose, with narrow nostrils that were as sensitive as those of a race-horse: an adventurous, pointing nose that would lead its owner into valiant lengths, but would never lead him into low enterprises. His eyes had a quick, perceptive look, so that he probably understood things speedily. And the kindly, forbearing look in them promised that his understanding would not be stiffened by harshness, that it would be accompanied by sympathy so keen that, were it not for the hint of humour they had, he might also have been mawkish, a sentimentalist too easily dissolved in tears. His thick eyebrows hung closely over his eyes and gave him a look of introspection that mitigated the shrewdness of his pointing nose. There was some weakness, but not much, in the full, projecting lower lip and the slightly receding chin that caused his short, tightened upper lip to look indrawn and strained; and the big, ungainly, jutting ears consorted oddly with the serious look of high purpose that marked his face in repose. It was as though Puck had turned poet and then had turned preacher. One looked at the fleshy lower lip and the jutting ears, and thought of a careless, impish creature; one looked at the shapely, pointing nose and the kindly, unflinching eyes, and thought of a man reckless of himself in the pursuit of some fine purpose.

When the news of his execution was proclaimed, a woman wept in the street.

'Ah, poor Tom MacDonagh,' she said. 'And he wouldn't have hurt a fly!'

I do not know what dreams these men had in their minds, but this much is certain, their was nothing unclean or mean about their motives. I think that they were foolish men, and I think that they did incalculable harm to their country; but whatever was their belief, they were prepared to suffer the hardest test for it – the test of death.

'We did not come here to surrender,' some of the rebels said to an envoy, carrying a white flag, who came to demand their surrender; 'we came here to die.' And when their stronghold was subsequently taken, only one man out of twenty-three was still alive, and he died soon afterward.

The rebellion was virtually over on the Saturday following Easter Monday, but for the best part of the succeeding week there was still some difficult work to be done in rounding up the snipers who had taken to the roofs of houses. In places like Merrion Square they were virtually immune from discovery. They could run along the roofs, hidden by parapets, and fire at the troops with a minimum chance of detection; but their position was a hopeless one. Death or discovery was inevitable, and in a few days the last of the snipers were taken.

About the middle of the second week I was able to get across O'Connell Bridge into O'Connell Street. The official name of O'Connell Street is Sackville Street. A soldier told me that Ypres was not much worse than O'Connell Street was. An American lady who had seen Louvain said that that town was not more battered and broken than the heart of Dublin. One saw a huddle of torn walls and twisted girders and rusty rails and stones and ashes. I went hurriedly to Marlborough Street, and found that the Abbey Theatre had been marvellously untouched, though the houses immediately facing it were in ruins. The Royal Hibernian Academy, where an exhibition of pictures was being held, was a heap of cinders. One had to walk warily because the ground was covered with hot ashes, and if one was not careful, one sank into them and was burned.

PART TWO

OUTSIDE DUBLIN

Michael Newell,
Irish Volunteers, Castlegar,
County Galway, 1916.[17]

On Holy Thursday night, 1916, Brian Molloy, Tom Ruane and I met George Nichols by appointment at Oranmore railway station. Nichols was travelling on the train from Dublin which arrived at Oranmore at 12 midnight. Nichols told us that the Rising was to start at 7 o'clock on Easter Sunday evening, and to convey that message immediately to Captain Alf Monahan, who at that time was 'on the run' at Cashla, Athenry. We went straight to Cashla, walking all the way, a distance of about six Irish miles. We gave Monahan the message; he did not seem one bit surprised. He then gave us our instructions. He told us that the Castlegar and Claregalway Companies were to join together and attack and capture the police hut at Lydecan, which was occupied by about five policemen. Having captured the hut and taken all arms, equipment, etc., we were to burn the hut, take the police prisoners and march to Loughgeorge, attack and capture the Police Barracks there which was garrisoned by about nine policemen. We were then to proceed to Kilcon and capture the Police Barracks there, which was also garrisoned by about nine men. Having made prisoners of the police in each Barracks we were, to handcuff them together, and march them at the head of the Volunteers into Galway

---

[17]   B.M.H., W.S. 342

City where we would link up with units front other areas and receive further instructions. On Good Friday night Captain Brian Molloy gave instructions for the Company to parade at 2 p.m. on Easter Sunday, bring all arms and equipment and two days' rations He also advised us to go to confession and to offer up Holy Communion on Easter Sunday for the freedom of Ireland.

On Holy Saturday morning I was making pike heads in my forge at Brierhill. I was finishing the last batch at about 12.30 when Fr. Feeney arrived. He gave us similar instructions as had been given to us by George Nichols. He also said that there was a possibility of arms being landed on the Connemara coast. While Fr. Feeney was in the forge a Sergeant and two R.I.C. men came along. When they saw the priest in the forge they did not come in but called me to go out to them. I said, 'anything you have to say to me, say it here,' the Sergeant said, 'have information that you are making pike heads and I warn you that if I catch you, you will be charged under the Defence of the Realm Act.' They then departed and almost immediately Micheál Ó Droighneáin of Spiddal came along and asked me for some pike heads. I at first refused as I wanted them for my own Company. Fr. Feeney requested me to give them; I then gave him about two dozen. I went to confession and received Holy Communion on Easter Sunday and. offered it up for the freedom of Ireland. The Company mobilised as instructed and marched to Carnmore crossroads, where we linked up with the Claregalway Company at about 6 p.m. Brian Molloy was in charge of the Castlegar Company and Nicholas Kyne was in charge of the Claregalway Company. The Castlegar Company was about sixty strong, between twenty and twenty-five wore armed with shotguns, the remainder had the pikes I made. We were instructed to 'stand-to' for further orders. After a short time we were told that operations were cancelled and marched back to Castlegar; Claregalway Company went to its own area. We were told to hold ourselves in readiness for an immediate mobilisation. As there was a wake in Castlegar practically the whole Company went to it.

On Easter Monday morning we collected some shotguns from farmers in the district. At about 4 a.m. on Tuesday, Pat Callanan ('the hare') and Joe Fleming arrived with instructions from Commandant

Mellows that the Rising was on and to mobilise the Company and to proceed to Oranmore where we were to join forces with the Oranmore, Clarinbridge and Maree Companies. Brian Molloy went with Pat Callanan to mobilise the Moycullen Company and on his return at about 5 p.m. on Tuesday we marched to the Carnmore Crossroads where we met the Claregalway Company. We continued in the direction of Oranmore, but on the way we were informed that the companies we were to link up with there had gone to Athenry. Captain Molloy sent Lieutenant Tom Newell and a Volunteer from Claregalway Company to Commandant Mellows at Athenry for instructions. Both companies marched to Carnmore where the Claregalway Company billeted in farmhouses and barns. The Castlegar Company billeted in Kiltullagh and sentries were placed on all roads. At about 3 a.m. on Wednesday, Captain Brian Molloy instructed me to go to Kiltullagh and bring the Castlegar Company to Carnmore. The Castlegar Company proceeded in the direction of Carnmore crossroads. Just as we reached the cross roads a dispatch was received from Commandant Mellows instructing Captain Molloy to proceed with both Companies to the Farmyard, Athenry, and to commandear food and transport. The Company was halted and Captain Molloy was giving instructions as to where horses, etc. were to be got. It was then about 5 a.m. on Wednesday. I noticed a girl on hill at Kiltullagh waving a white apron, apparently in order to attract our attention. She was Miss Sheila (Bina) King. I looked to see what was wrong and saw a number of motor cars about half a mile away coming in our direction from Galway City.

We at first thought it was the Galway City Volunteers coming to join with us. Captain Molloy ordered us to take cover behind the walls. Just as we had taken cover, fire was opened on us. We proceeded to about one hundred yards from our position and then halted. The enemy advanced on foot on our position, firing all the time. Captain Molloy ordered us to open fire which we did, but the enemy fire was so intense and the bullets striking the top of the walls, we were compelled to keep down, and we were only able to take an occasional shot. The enemy advanced up to the cross roads and Constable Whelan was pushed by District Inspector Herd, up to the wall which was about four feet high, the District Inspector standing behind Whelan and holding him by the collar of his tunic. Constable Whelan shouted, 'surrender, boys, I know ye all'. Whelan was shot dead and the District Inspector fell also and lay motionless on the ground. The enemy then made an attempt to outflank our position but were beaten back. The enemy then retreated and continued to fire until well out of range of our shotgun. They got back into the cars and went in the direction of Oranmore. We had about sixty men at the crossroads, about thirty of them had shotguns and the remainder had pikes. I believe the enemy had thirteen cars with five or six men in each car. We suffered no casualties. The enemy had one killed and I believe five or six wounded. The Company then fell in and marched across country to the Farmyard, Athenry.

As we arrived near the Farmyard between 10 and 11 a.m. we had to take cover as the R.I.C. were firing on the Farmyard from the railway bridge. This attack was beaten off and we continued into the Farmyard. At about 4 o'clock that evening (Wednesday) the Brigade under Commandant Mellows marched by road to Moyode Castle where we billeted until Friday evening. Sentries were placed at various points. Commandant Mellows had the general alarm sounded often so as to keep us on the alert. At about 2 o'clock on Friday morning the alarm sounded and the whole Garrison assembled in the yard. Commandant Mellows instructed each Company to 'stand-to' attention on its own. Fr. Feeney told us to remove our cape and to say an Act of Contrition; he then gave us General Absolution. Various rumours were continually floating round the camp. One rumour was to the effect that strong British forces were advancing, on our position from Loughrea and Galway City. At about 3 or 4 o'clock on Friday evening we marched to Lime Park, travelling along the bye-road. It was near midnight when we reached Lime Park. I went to have a sleep as I had very little rest during the previous week. A few minutes later I was awakened by Jim Feeney (brother of Fr. Feeney) who told me we were to disband. I went 'on the run' with Brian Molloy. We stood with friends in various parts of Galway, but at the end of a week we were captured. I was brought to Galway Jail and later tranferred to Richmond Barracks, Dublin.

Áine Ní Riain,
25 Upper Gardiner Street,
Cumann na mBan, Tullamore,
1915.[18]

O n Easter Saturday I came up to Dublin by train to stay with my sister in St. Joseph Street. I had the intention of going home to Longford on Sunday, but there was so much excitement in Dublin that nobody took any interest in my plans, so I gave up the idea. On Sunday I went out for a walk with my sister. On Sunday night we went down to the Keating Branch of the Gaelic League. There were not many people there and I did not know any of them except Effie Taaffe. I was not aware that P.H. Pearse was there. There was a lot of talk about the countermanding order of MacNeill and there seemed to have been a lot of running in all directions all day. I think the Cumann na mBan had decided to go out the mountains on the Monday, but I heard no talk of a Rising for that day or, if I did, I did not understand it. On Monday morning the Cumann na mBan mobilised in Palmerston Place near the Broadstone. I went up with my sister. I don't know if they had any instructions at that time about the day's activities. If they had, I was not told. I left them there and I came away with the intention of visiting a friend in Gray Street, near

---

[18] B.M.H., W.S. 887

Meath Street. I was waiting for a tram at Parnell Street to take me to the quays when some shots were fired. That was the shooting at the Lancers. There was terrible confusion and running about and I gave up the idea of visiting my friend. I returned to St Joseph's Street. All the people there were standing at doors. Some were giving out about the Volunteers, and some saying nothing. I stayed at Mrs Cleary's in St Joseph's Street for the rest of the evening.

Her husband was a Volunteer and he had mobilised on Sunday, but he went to the Fairyhouse Races on Monday and did not get the mobilisation order for that day. His train from the races only brought them to Liffey Junction and they had to make their way home as best they could. That evening my sister and a friend, Emily Elliott, came in and got ready to go out that night to Reis' Chambers, which was an outpost of the G.P.O. H.Q. They told me the password 'Wireless'. The following morning I got up very early and, after Mass, Mrs Cleary and myself were standing at the door and there was a girl living opposite – Margaret Derham – who was in Cumann na mBan. She was very anxious to see her young brother who had been mobilised with his section of the Volunteers. Mrs Cleary said to me, 'This is a chance for you now. You can go with her.' We went down to Reis' Chambers, gave the password and got in. We found that her brother was not there but at the Four Courts or some other post. She went away and I did not see her again. This was about 7 a.m. My sister, the Elliotts and a crowd of Cumann na mBan and of Volunteers were there filling up the small space. During the day a message came from the Pour Courts asking for some Cumann na mBan girls. My sister and her friends went there, as most of the Volunteers from the North side that they knew were there.

Later that day most of the people in Reis' Chambers went into the Hibernian Bank and we with them. We got busy then filling baths of water and sterilising it for First-Aid instruments, etc. They were afraid the water would be cut off. There was one huge bath of sterilised water and I was nearly killed by Mary Lawless for dipping a jug into it and destroying the whole lot. I was in terror of her ever afterwards. At this stage I met a very marvellous Mrs English, with whom I got pally (I have to thank her for my certificates for service in Easter Week). Before nightfall two fellows came across from Reis' Chambers and asked for two girls to go back there to prepare meals, etc., as they had no girl at all. Mrs English immediately volunteered and I said I would go with her. When we had said that the fellow said 'Remember now, it is a death trap.' My heart fell to my boots but I did not pretend anything. We went and tidied up the place. I remember some of the people. They were Captain Paddy McGrath, now dead, who was at one time Works Manager of the *Irish Press*; Captain Wearer and Seán McGarry. The wireless was in operation upstairs – John O'Connor (Blimey of the London Irish) was at it all the night with Fergus Kelly. I got to know Blimey well later.

There was a good lot of shooting that night and we were all taking cover. Mrs English was giving out the Rosary and we were answering it. During the night Seán McGarry's sister-in-law came in. I think Jeskon was the name. My memory tells me that some of the British occupied McBirney's roof during the night, because the boys were always looking over there. At daybreak things got quiet and Mrs English cooked a breakfast for the men. She gave them chops and we drank tea. During the morning I don't know how it came about that we girls were leaving and going back to the Hibernian Bank. What was going on there was that they were boring into the next building, a chemist's shop which is now Hamilton Longs. The place was choked with dust. All that time there was dreadful shooting from the *Helga*. We could not hear each other talking. I think that was the reason for our evacuation.

I don't know how it came about but I found myself and another girl carrying a zinc bath full of food from Reis' Chambers across to the G.P.O. with our heads bent down to the ground. We did this at least twice and were admitted through the side door in Princes Street. Then a crowd of us met at the building next the Hibernian Bank. There was a priest there – I think a Father Gleeson from Gardiner Street. He said if any of us wished to go home to the North side we could get through with him. Some of them went, including Mrs English, to report home and to see how things were going on there. But they never got back because a cordon had been closed around the area. I afterwards found out that Mrs English linked up with the Ashbourne crowd.

I went over finally to stay in the G.P.O. with the other girls of the crowd. We were employed upstairs in the restaurant where there was a huge range. I remember Desmond Fitzgerald who was in charge of the cooking arrangements. I remember the British Tommy – a Dublin man – who was cooking all the time and joking with the girls. He was in great humour and he had a rosary beads round his neck. I don't know where all the religious objects that all the people in the G.P.O. were wearing came from.

Jim Ryan and Phyllis were there. Miss Gavan Duffy was in charge of all the girls. I remember Brian O'Higgins too. There were British prisoners there – some of them officers – to whom we brought meals. Things went on like that all day and night. I don't think we lay down at all that night. We had only arrived in the G.P.O. when we got the news that Thomas Weafer was killed in the Hibernian Bank. I should have told you that before. I heard afterwards that Leslie Price was with him when he was dying.

On Thursday it was much the same only that the bombarding was much heavier and I thought the place would come down around us every minute. That was the day the Imperial Hotel and other buildings near it came down. That night some of us at least lay down on mattresses in the basement. I was wakened up by the moans of a wounded man...

Some Cumann na mBan girls were helping with the bandages, etc...On Friday morning Patrick Pearse sent for all of us girls and he made a very nice speech to us. He compared us to the women of Limerick. I often regret I did not take down the speech in shorthand. He said he wished that everyone of us who was not qualified in First Aid should leave, as the fighting would get very severe and it would probably come to using bayonets to fight their way out. Leslie Price took charge of those of us who were to leave. She carried a Red Cross flag. There were quite a number who remained – Tilly Simpson, Margaret McElroy and others. I think Tilly was with Liam Clarke when he was wounded. We came out through the wall of a building into Henry Street. Seán McDermott and Patrick Pearse were standing inside the wall of the building and shook hands with each one of us as we passed out. I think the building was the new Coliseum Cinema. Leslie brought us down Henry Street to Jervis Street Hospital on the suggestion of Father O'Flanagan, who had been down there already. It was full to overflowing.

Daniel Tuite,
Irish Volunteers
Dundalk, 1914 –[19]

On Holy Saturday night at a parade in the Boyle O'Reilly Hall we got orders for the mobilisation on Easter Sunday morning after 8 a.m. Mass. We were to have a feed before mobilising, We mobilised on the street opposite the Hall. Some of the men had arms on this mobilisation. I did not see much arms at the mobilisation but when we marched off up the Ardee Road to the Workhouse at Ballybarrack we were joined by another contingent of the Dundalk Volunteers. Some of these Volunteers carried arms especially the men from Kilkearley locality. I saw a fair number of rifles amongst the men then. I had no arms then. All the men carried rifles for at least one day. There were a few jarveys with horse cars along with us. There were about seventy men marched from Ballybarrack.

We marched out the Ardee Road and during the march we made use of the cars by taking short rides alternatively on them. There was only accommodation on the cars for about a quarter of the men marching.

When we arrived in Ardee we were halted in military formation and remained standing there for about a half hour. Paddy Hughes and Domhnall O'Hannigan were walking about in our vicinity. Later

---

[19] B.M.H., W.S., 337

Hughes and O'Hannigan came to us with rifles and distributed them to some of the men. I was handed one of the rifles and a quantity of ammunition. The ammunition was loose and I put it in my pockets, I got about twenty rounds of ammunition. I knew how to load the rifle but I had got no rifle drill before the rifle was handed out to me. I was not told to load the rifle. About nine men joined us in Ardee from Dunleer district.

From Ardee we marched in the direction of Collon, through Collon and when about half way between Collon and Slane we stopped on the roadside for a rest. When resting Sean MacEntee came to me and asked me if I would like to go back to Dundalk. He told me he knew I was working for Mr McDonald, Contractor, and that the Volunteers would not be proceeding much further that evening. I told him that I would remain with the Volunteers and do whatever the main body did. He did not tell me anything about the countermanding order which I now know he carried to the point at which we were resting. I saw a good many of the Volunteers going home at this point. When we resumed our march towards Slane we had forty to forty-five men remaining. I heard that some of the men who left us were asked to do some work in Dundalk, mostly in the line of dispatch work, for Miss Matthews or dispatches left at the Boyle O'Reilly Hall.

We arrived in Slane about dark that evening. We had a feed in Slane in relays as the house where we got the food could not accommodate many of us. When in Slane we were accompanied by Sergeants Wymes and Connolly. Both of these men were with us continually from when we left Dundalk. We remained in Slane moving about in groups for a time. We had a feeling that matters were at sixes and sevens. The whole outlook was uncertain and we were just waiting to see what we would be told to do.

Whilst we were waiting in Slane late at night, Sean MacEntee left us. Shortly after he went away we were forming up again in military formation and marched back in the direction of Collon. It was raining very heavily on our journey to Collon. From Collon we took the road for Dunleer, marched through Dunleer where the Dunleer men left us and the Dundalk men continued on through Castlebellingham on to Lurgangreen four miles from Dundalk.

At this place Sean MacEntee met us on a motor bicycle coming from Dundalk and told us the Rising was on in Dublin…When on guard duty we could hear the heavy firing from the gun boats shelling Dublin. When Sunday came there was no Mass for us. The Rosary was recited every night. Our strength all told – Louth and Dunboyne men in Tyrellstown House was about sixty men. We were daily waiting for word to advance to Dublin or otherwise. When we were about five days in the place reports of an alarming, kind came to us. We knew then that it was impossible to get into Dublin and dangerous to remain where we were. Word was brought to us that the Soldiers were to attack us in Tyrellstown House that very night – 1st May. Our leaders, knowing the folly of trying to defend the place with the men and arms at our disposal decided to evacuate. We quickly and silently mustered, collected every thing belonging to us that we could carry and started on our long journey through fields across hedges and rivers plodding along without complaint. We had a guide who knew the country. He did not dare to take us the direct way we were travelling but roundabout routes to baffle the soldiers who we expected were following us. We stopped occasionally to listen for sounds of pursuers. At those stops D. O'Hannagan would count us as we filed past, him and when he satisfied himself that 'all was correct' we proceeded. Our progress was slow, getting over or through hedges, etc. encumbered as we were by rifles and equipment in the darkness. We avoided gates and roads as much as possible. At some of the deep drains we got across by means of planks.

The country we were crossing was all big ranch land and houses were a great distance apart. We were beginning to get very fatigued and it seemed that we could go little further when we saw a light in a house. We proceeded to the house and were delighted to find that it was the house of one of the girls who had been so helpful to us during our stay in Tyrellstown House. We were welcomed with kindness by the occupants who knew by this time that the 'Cause' was lost; that mothers in a short time would see their sons arrested, sisters lose their brothers, but they welcomed us. Heaps of bread was baked ready for us, pots of tea prepared and after a short time we had a welcome feed. We thanked our good friends and hurriedly bade them good bye and resumed our march to get as far as possible during darkness. It was on leaving this house we parted with the Dunboyne men. We had not gone far on our resumed march when we found out that we were close to our former camping place, the old Barn we had occupied on our journey to Tyrellstown House. Some of us suggested that we should go there and rest awhile but Paddy Hughes knowing the great danger of delay under the circumstances decided to keep going. Our guide, who had the instinct of 'an Indian' and never once led us astray, now left the road and we entered a dense wood. Our progress here was slow but we came out on the other side to flat open country. Our guide here pointed out to us a farm cottage and we staggered towards it. When we arrived at the cottage our guide told us it belonged to him, was unoccupied and could accommodate us all. We were not long in the cottage when we were all fast asleep. After a few hours sleep we got up again, we all looked deplorable objects.

Our hands and clothes torn with wire and hedges we passed through the previous night, our boots filled with mud and our legs soaked to the knees from wading through streams. Our guide got a fire going. He procured food and after a feed we did not feel so bad – over a smoke we could even laugh at the hardships of the previous night march. About mid-day a messenger brought us the alarming news that the British at daylight that morning had surrounded Tyrellstown House and when they found it vacant had come after us to the old Barn and not finding us there were searching the surrounding district. We later got a message that the soldiers were coming in the direction of the cottage where we were resting. We made preparations to receive them by taking up positions for defence We waited in expectancy of what was to come but God was on our side as the soldiers passed along the main road and the cottage where we waited was, only a few hundred, yards from where they passed, on a bye road.

After the soldiers passed we gathered around our leader Paddy Hughes to discuss what should now be done, He, poor fellow, advised a general disbandment for all who desired to go before it was too late. We all agreed to his decision. About 4 p.m. that evening after dumping our arms and equipment we started to move off in batches of six or seven to try for home as best we could. There were a few of our men decided to remain and go with Paddy Hughes and share his fate. About 6 p.m. a comrade and I took leave of Paddy Hughes and we started for home. We kept to the highroad all through and travelled late into the night. It was threatening rain and very dark. My comrade took a weak turn and lay down. This would be about 2 a.m. After a short time my comrade to whom I could give little help said he was feeling better and we again started off but had to travel much slower. We were tottering for loss of sleep and fatigue. I had to help my comrade along. When daylight came we decided to keep going and did so. We arrived to within six miles of Drogheda. We were warned before we left our last resting place that the bridges near Drogheda were guarded by the British so to avoid capture we turned left about two miles south of Drogheda which led us near the town by a back way. We did not enter the town as our appearance would give us away. We went into a roadside bed to rest for a few hours. About 8 a.m. we arranged to move into town, one of us going in advance of the other. I travelled in front and I first saw about procuring a feed for both of us. When my companion arrived we were able to go to the place I had arranged for a feed and have a good breakfast. We had a wash up and brushed our clothes. We remained in Drogheda about two hours and after meeting a friend we knew who told us that delaying in Drogheda was dangerous we left the town avoiding the main road, I going first. When about two miles North of Drohgeda I waited until my comrade came up with me and we proceeded together. We passed a few inns but did not stop. We purchased some food and came to near Dunleer on our left. We went to a friend's house near here for food and a rest. On our way to the friend's house we met two of the Dunleer men who had parted with us on Easter Monday and they told us how to get to the friend's house without attracting attention. At the friend's house we got a good feed and were told how to get, by a bye road directly to Castlebellingham. We arrived at Castlebellingham Station about 10 p.m. We had to be careful here as the R.I.C. were guarding the station and railway line. We took to the fields at Castlebellingham and lost ourselves and several times found ourselves near the Station having travelled in circles through the fields. We got on a narrow road after we felt apparently lost in the fields and unfortunately this road did not take us in Dundalk direction but across country. After wasting some hours in fruitless wandering we arrived within sight of the Distillery Chimney in Dundalk. Our wandering in circles around Castlebellingham was fortunate in a way as had we not gone astray we could have arrived in Dundalk about 3 a.m. and have been in our homes when the police and military carried out a big round up of all the volunteers in Dundalk. When we arrived in town I parted with my comrade in Chapel Lane. I have never seen him since and I went to a house in Mill Street which I reached at 6 a.m. in the last stages of physical exhaustion. I immediately went to bed.

I was awakened from a sound sleep to be told that soldiers and police were looking for me at my home at 3 a.m. that morning. I was also told of the arrests in various parts of the town and parades through the streets in handcuffs to the Courthouse and elsewhere. Having no desire to be forced through the town in such a manner I got out of bed and proceeded to Ann St. R.I.C. Barracks and enquired there if the police were looking for me.

Commandant Michael Gray, Drumcondra, Dublin. Irish Volunteers/I.R.B., Maryborough, Port Laoise.[20]

Ned Fleming was sent down by Pearse in the same way as Liam Mellows was sent to Galway and Mulcahy was sent to County Dublin. I understood that we were to operate under de Loughrey in Kilkenny, and that they were to join us there.

On the Thursday night the equipment for the demolition of the railway was collected, cross-cuts, hatchets, and all that sort of stuff. It was then we bought shotguns in the local hardware shop, the foreman of which was in the Volunteers. We bought as many shotguns as we could use, as well as shotgun ammunition. I remember that pikes were being seriously talked about. I believe that the only thing that prevented some of the Volunteers being armed with pikes was that we had no blacksmith in our confidence.

On Thursday night the stuff was shifted out to Lalor's Mills, the home of Lar and Tom Brady, two members of the organisation. They had a mill and a farm not far from the railway line and all the stuff was brought out there. I believe that stuff was shifted to a place called Colt Wood which was on the line, on Easter Saturday evening.

---

20 B.M.H., W.S. 489

On that Saturday night we met in St. Patrick's Hall, in the town, to have a final check-up, and I believe we formally elected Eamon Fleming as the leader. Final arrangements for the following morning, Easter Sunday, were decided on. Briefly these were that a party of six Volunteers under the leadership of Paddy Ramsbottom were to cut the line at Colt Wood at 7 p.m. on Sunday. Another small party, consisting of myself, a man named Walsh, Commandant Fleming and a stranger from Dublin, were to meet south of Athy in order to destroy telephone communications at the same time on Sunday evening. As arranged, we met at the appointed time and place outside Athy. There was some slight disappointment about the tools and the number of personnel who were to take part in the operation. In any case we cut the wires to the best of our ability until Fleming was satisfied. I have an idea that time was considered important. Fleming ultimately called the thing off, I think, and we proceeded to join the other party outside Maryborough.

We slept in a schoolhouse that night, and it was some time early on Monday morning before we joined up with Paddy Ramsbottom's party. His party had by this time cut the railway as instructed. The Coltwood party had started the work of demolition punctually at 7 p.m. on Easter Sunday. People who came along the railway line during the course of this operation were held as prisoners, escorted to their homes and warned that they were not to go out again that night or to give any information. Heavy rain had set in while the operations were in progress. They had been told to guard the cut on the line for some time. The party remained on guard at the spot and took shelter in the wood beside the railway. A man came along carrying a lamp. Presumably he was a railway employee making an inspection of the line in consequence of the failure of the block signal system between Portlaoighise and Abbeyleix stations. One of the Volunteers on the job was actually a linesman, and the whole thing was done under his direction. The idea of breaking the signal system was to prevent the entry of any train on the section of the line that was put out of action. Telegraph wires were also cut there. The railway employee was called on to halt. According to our men he did not halt and they fired over his head. According to them he extinguished his lamp and escaped in the darkness.

The demolition party stayed guarding the cut for some hours. I know they were ordered to stay there for a certain length of time but I do not know for how long. They were drenched to the skin that night and they retired to Bradys' place, Lalor's Mills, which was not far away. We arrived there the next morning. They were expecting word to join up with Scollop Gap, but nothing happened and we remained together under arms. A sister of the Bradys was sent to Maryborough to find out news about the Rising elsewhere, but there was no news. She brought home a copy of Monday's *Independent*. I have a very vivid recollection of the railway man who was with us. and who was an anti-capitalist, burning the 'Independent' and cursing Martin Murphy who was responsible, he thought, for hiding the fact that the Rebellion had taken place on the Sunday. He seemed convinced that the Volunteers in Dublin had actually gone out. I had not read the *Sunday Independent* before mobilising on Easter Sunday, and was unaware of MacNeill's orders cancelling the mobilisations for that day. My distinct recollection is that at an I.R.B. meeting on Easter Saturday night, it was suggested that there might be a cancellation of the mobilisation order in the following morning's press, but if there was that we were not to take any notice of it... There had been no communication, so it was decided to try and get in touch with Kilkenny and Carlow. Eamon Fleming and Walsh who had gone with me to Athy originally started off on bicycles to Borne, County Carlow, but they were not able to contact anybody who could give them information...Some of us were more or less confined to Bradys' place because it was known we were missing from Maryboro' and if we were spotted by the police or their agents we would have been arrested.

Jim Ramsbottom was sent to Kilkenny to interview a Mr Kiely, who was the contact there at the time. Unfortunately Kiely had been arrested that morning and had died suddenly in the local barracks the same day, and Ramsbottom had to come back without any information. We remained together for the week believing that Dublin had come out, although over twelve hours late, and believing that although the Rising had been delayed it would carry on. We considered that we should remain in a state of mobilisation until we got definite orders where we were to go. However, on the following

Monday morning it was decided that Fleming would go to Dublin and find out as far as he could what was happening there. When Fleming arrived in Dublin he saw a Mr McEvoy, an old I.R.B. man from the Fenian organisation, but all Mr McEvoy could tell him was that all the leaders had been arrested and that the Rising was over. We did not accept the view that the Rising was finished even at that stage and we decided to hold together for a couple of weeks longer. We thought there was a possibility that the Rising was not over and we wanted to hold on until we were sure. We held on for about two weeks longer although it was fairly hopeless. We had tried Carlow, Kilkenny and Dublin and we could not make contact with anybody, and all we could do was to hold on in the hope that something would turn up. Fleming again went to Dublin at the end of this time, but the plain truth was that the Rebellion was over and done with. One of the local clergy made contact with the Bradys to try and get us to surrender to the police, but we refused. We decided that we would dump our arms and go on the run in preference, which we did.

Thomas Kelly, Co. Leitrim.
Irish Volunteers, Co. Tyrone
1914–1916.[21]

I joined the I.R.B. in Donoughmore in 1914. I was introduced by Joe Carbury. My father, W.J. Kelly, was also a member…A Capt. McRory, an ex-American officer, attended our parades and gave instructions and drilled us. About the end of 1914 I went to Scotland. I met James Tamoney from Coalisland in Motherwell. I attended meetings in Glasgow in the Sinn Fein Hall in Anne St. I met I.R.B. men there but never attended an I.R.B. meeting. I returned to Ireland for the O'Donovan Rossa funeral in August 1915 and after the funeral I returned again to Motherwell. I remained in Scotland up to shortly before the Rising. When I returned home I attended regular drills and parades in Dungannon area. We occasionally travelled to Donoughmore and practised on targets with .22 rifles. The leader in Donoughmore in those days was a man named James McElvogue. He was originally a leading Hibernian and was President of the Donoughmore Division A.O.H. when he joined the I.R.B. He remained in the Hibernians and when the split came he took his whole division of the Hibernians into the Volunteers and we got the use of the Hibernian Hall. Some time before Easter Week Tom Clarke sent a supply of rifles to Donoughmore; those were some

---

21 B.M.H., W.S. 378

of the Howth rifles. I can not now remember how many we had in 1916, probably twenty to thirty. The Hibernians in Dungannon had rifles which they got through John Redmond's organisation which were of Italian make and useless. We had not control of those which were stored in their Hall in Dungannon. On Saturday of Holy Week I was told to accompany a man named Hamill to Trewamoy and board the train from Belfast there and travel on the train on which the Belfast men were travelling on to Dungannon that night. When the Belfast men arrived in Dungannon we took them along to the Drill Hall in Dungannon. Later, all the Belfast men marched from Dungannon to Coalisland. It was only on Saturday when I was told to go to Trewamoy that I knew that a Rising was near. I got no further orders on Saturday night and on Sunday morning I travelled by pony and trap to Coalisland. I cannot remember who was with me for sure. I expect it must have been my father and James McElvogue. When we arrived in Coalisland we went to St Patrick's Hall where we met Volunteers from Belfast, Benburb, Coalisland and Donoughmore. The Volunteers, as far as I can remember, were standing about talking and discussing what should be done. I was speaking to Archie Heron and he was talking about the possibility of getting to Dublin. About midday on Sunday a messenger arrived with a dispatch. There was talk before the messenger arrived that the mobilisation was called off, but apparently nothing definite was known until this man arrived on a motorbike with Eoin MacNeill's countermanding orders. After the countermanding orders arrived nearly all the Belfast Volunteers formed up and marched from Coalisland in Cookstown direction and got a train there for Belfast. I remained that evening in Coalisland and, as far as I could see, all the Tyrone Volunteers there demobilised.

I went home on Sunday night, and on Monday I kept moving about in Dungannon. I was in and out to Jack McElvogue of Dungannon who was then I.R.B. Centre there, expecting some orders or dispatchee from Dublin. Nothing came.

On Tuesday, Seamus Dempsey arrived at Jack McElvogue's with a message to mobilise the Volunteers and to proceed to Donoughmore. I went around all the Volunteers in Dungannon and mobilised them. We procured the two or three rifles then stored in Dungannon and proceeded to James McElvogue's place at Tullydraw, Donoughmore. That night we joined up with the Donoughmore Volunteers and marched to Carrickmore, eleven or twelve miles distant.

When we arrived at Carrickmore there was no person to meet us We got a man named Daly out of his bed and he told us that the mobilisation was off. I cannot remember if Daly went away to find out the position before he told us all was off or that he knew it before we arrived. Daly was a prominent Volunteer at the time. We didn't start from Carrickmore until some time late on Wednesday morning. On this journey to Carrickmore we all carried rifles and a supply of ammunition. When waiting at a shop on the road near Carrickmore, two R.I.C. walked up and down the road past us several times. They bid us the time of the morning. We started for home and I arrived in Dungannon on Wednesday about 1 p.m. Before we dispersed we dumped the arms at Largalea near Galbally. We left them with an old woman who lived alone. The Galbally Volunteers were then to take charge of them and have them safely dumped, which I know they did. On Thursday, about midday, a message came to Jack McElvogue's. I got this message to procure a car to take a lady to Carrickmore, who desired to contact Dr Pat McCartan. I got a motor car and a driver in Dungannon. The driver was Thomas McGuigan, an I.R.B. man. We proceeded to Peter McGrath's, Derrytresk, and picked up the lady, Miss Nora Connolly, and James Tamoney of Coalisland. I was told that Miss Connolly was armed. It was coming on dusk when we arrived at Dr McCartan's place. Before we arrived there we met military lorries at Pomeroy who, we heard later, had been raiding McCartan's house.

When we arrived at McCartan's house we met Dr McCartan and his brother, Johnnie. Miss Connolly, when speaking to Doctor McCartan, urged him to do something. I understood from her manner that she had orders for Dr McCartan. Miss Connolly remained in Dr McCartan's and we returned towards Dungannon. We left Tamoney in Coalisland on our way back. We were held up by two R.I.C. in Coalisland. Tamoney jumped out of the car on the opposite side from the R.I.C. and boarded the mail car and got away undetected. We were questioned as to where we were coming from. The driver told the policemen that I was in Omagh visiting a sister of mine who was in hospital there and they let us through. When we came near Dungannon I got out of the car as I feared the police in Coalisland would have a check up on the driver's yarn to them and send word into Dungannon police to pick us up. I walked into Dungannon and when I arrived there I met Jack Shields, Benburb, and we decided to raid St Patrick's Hall, Dungannon, for the Nationalist Volunteer rifles. Jack, Tom Hamill, Peter Byrne and myself carried out the raid. We carried away all the rifles in the Hall and hid them in a store in Brannagan's yard in Dungannon. Hamill came into town the next day with a pony and cart and removed them to his place in the country where they were properly hid.

On 5th My 1916, I and my father were arrested at our own house, taken to the local R.I.C. Bks. and later to Armagh R.I.C. Bks. After a time there we were transferred to Richmond Bks. in Dublin. When in Richmond I saw Sean McDermott. He was executed shortly afterwards. About 7th or 8th June I was removed with a batch of prisoners to Wandsworth Prison. After a month there we were removed to Frongoch. I was taken from Frongoch to Wormwood Scrubs to go before the Commission to be questioned on our membership of what was then an illegal organisation.

I was released at Xmas 1916 and returned to my home in Dungannon.

Patrick Callanan,
Craughwell, Co. Galway.
Brigade Chief of Scouts
1915–1916.[22]

Late spring or early summer 1915, Liam Mellows came as Chief Organiser for Galway. Shortly after his arrival, Galway was organised into a Brigade of four Battalions. The Battalions were, Galway, Athenry, Loughrea and Gort. Larry Lardiner was appointed Brigade O/C. I was Brigade Chief of scouts, which appointment I held up to and during the Rising. I also maintained my connection with the Clarinbridge Company. Eamon Corbett was appointed O/C. Athenry Battalion…

At about 2 p.m. on Easter Monday, Fr. Feeney rushed into Walsh's with the news that Dublin was out since 12 noon. The local Company was mobilised. Mellows sent me and Joe Fleming to instruct several Companies to mobilise imiediately in their own areas and to get in touch with him immediately they had done so. I mobilised Maree, Oranmore, Claregalway and Castlegar Companies. I was unable to get in touch with anyone in Galway city. I called to Pádraig Thornton, Captain of the Moycullen Company. He promised to mobilise his Company, but failed to do so; he also failed to send word to Micheál

---

22 B.M.H., W.S. 347

Ó Droighneáin, Captain of the Spiddal Company, as he promised to do. I returned to Clarinbridge with Joe Fleming at about 2 a.m. on Tuesday. I met Mellows and the Clarinbridge Company proceeding along the road in the direction of Oranmore. Mellows instructed me to go back and bring the Castlegar and Claregalway Companies to Oranmore and meet him there. When I arrived back at Oranmore with the two Companies, we found the British holding the bridge. We were informed that Mellows and the main body had gone to the Agricultural Station, Athenry. We returned to Carnmore Village at about 8 p.m. on Tuesday and having placed sentries, billeted for the night.

At about 4 a.m. on Wednesday about eight cars with police and special Constables were observed approaching from the direction of Galway. The Volunteers opened fire on them and they returned the fire. The cars advanced to the Carnmore Cross roads; they halted a short distance from where a small number of Volunteers were. The police called on the Volunteers to surrender. The Volunteers again opened fire, killing one policeman and wounding a few others. The police got into the ears and retreated in the direction of Oranmore. I was not present at this engagement; it was the sound of the shooting that awakened me. Immediately after this fight the two Companies proceeded across country to the Agricultural Station, Athenry.

Soon after our arrival there a Council of War was held at which the following were Fr. Feeney, Liam Mellows, Eamon Corbett, Larry Lardiner, Matty Niland, Tom Ruane, Dick Murphy. At the meeting Tom Ruane suggested that we should break up into small columns and fight the police as we would meet them. The meeting was unanimously against doing so. It was decided to move to Moyode Castle. Mellows instructed me and Willie Newell of Castlegar Company to go to Moycullen and bring the Moycullen Company to Moyode as they were supposed to have forty shotguns which would be of great use. When leaving the Agricultural station in Athenry, Mellows said to me he would never yield till the last hope was gone, as likely help would soon come, and Limerick and Clare would mobilise at the end of the week, which they did not. Willie Newell and I went to Moycullen but we could not find Thornton – he had disappeared. On the way back to Moyode I met Fr. Moran, P.P.,

Claregalway, at Carnmore. He gave me two long Webley revolvers. I sent them on to Moyode. When I got as far as Bushfield about seven miles from Moyode, I discovered that a large number of false reports were being sent out to Mellows at Moyode. I set up an outpost there consisting of Thomas Furey, Roger Furey, Pat Flanagan and myself. We had two shotguns and a revolver between us, ten or twelve shotgun cartridges and six rounds of revolver ammunition. I sent word to Mellows giving him the correct details as to the number of British troops in Galway City and informing him that there was no danger at all from this side, and asking him for further instructions. Mellows sent back word to remain where I was, and if any British troops should arrive, to comminicate with him immediately and to barricade the roads so as to delay their advance.

We remained at Bushfield all Friday, and late that evening we got word that the Volunteers were likely to move that night. Not having received any information from Moyode, we decided at 3 a.m. on Saturday to go there. We had gone about one mile when we met some Volunteers who told us that they had been disbanded. I instructed the few men I had with me to go home also. On Sunday I went 'on the run', and in August, 1916, I escaped to America with Eamon Corbett.

Michael Spillane,
Michael J. O'Sullivan
Killarney Coy. I.V. I.R.B.[23]

On Holy Thursday, 20th April, 1916, a dispatch carrier named Carroll, now dead, a native of North Kerry, arrived in Killarney from Dublin and gave Michael Spillane despatches to be delivered to His Lordship, Most Rev. Dr Mangan, Bishop of Kerry. Carroll also had despatches for Austin Stack, Tralee. Carroll stated that they were very short of reliable men at headquarters to bring messages to the provinces, and that the train had been searched three times for him. Michael Spillane delivered the messages to the Bishop, but had no knowledge, then or afterwards, of their contents.

Austin Stack had sent a message to Killarney that day for someone to come to Tralee to see him. Michael J. O'Sullivan went and took Carroll with him to Stack, to whom Carroll delivered his despatches. After Carroll left, O'Sullivan had a conference with Stack and Paddy Cahill. Stack then told O'Sullivan that a boat with arms was due to arrive in Fenit on Sunday morning and that a pilot had been arranged for at Leary's Island. He said the Rising was timed for Easter Sunday night. There was a long discussion on the questions of having a train in Fenit at the right time, the number of wagons that would be needed, the time it would take to unload the boat, the number of men necessary for the unloading, and similar matters.

23 B.M.H., W.S. 132

O'Sullivan understood that the arms were for distribution in Kerry, Cork, Limerick, Clare and Galway, and that the Kerry Brigade would be responsible for the safe delivery of the main portion of the cargo at Newcastle West by rail, afterwards distributing a portion of the cargo at Cork and Kerry. All Officers were to avoid arrest. The Killarney Battalion would not be engaged in the distribution at the arms. The orders for the Battalion were to cut the cable wires which ran from Valentia through Killarney at midnight on Easter Sunday night, then join forces with Castleisland, move towards Newcastle West and await further orders.

O'Sullivan asked Stack a number of questions about the arms and the boat. In reply Stack said he thought there would be a number of machine guns, but did not know if there would be men to man them. He said everything would be alright about the boat and that the train was to be commandeered. O'Sullivan finally asked if the orders were definite and specific and Stack said, 'You come over again on Sunday morning.' The conference lasted about two hours.

O'Sullivan arrived back in Killarney about 9.30 p.m. on the same night and went direct to the Volunteer Hall in High Street where Spillane was drilling the Killarney Company, He told Spillane the substance of his discussion with Stack and Cahill, and Spillane issued orders that no men were to leave town for the week-end.

After the parade was over 'An Seabhac' arrived. Spillane and O'Sullivan discussed the matter with him. Stack had given orders that everything was to be kept secret, but Spillane, O'Sullivan and 'An Seabhac' had always shared confidences. 'An Seabhac' was thinking of going, to Dublin next day, and Spillane told him what Carroll had said about the shortage of reliable messengers in Dublin. 'An Seabhac' went to Dublin on Good Friday, passed through Killarney on his way to Tralee on Easter Saturday and returned to Killarney on Easter Sunday morning. No orders were received on Friday or Saturday. Preparations were made for the mobilisation on Easter Sunday night. Volunteers were ordered to stand by and not leave the town, to see that their arms were in perfect order, and to be ready to parade at short notice with twenty-four hours rations. It was decided that the Listry Company would out the cables on the Killorglin–Killarney Road, and that the Killarney Company would break up the instruments in the Killarney Post Office. Stack had given no instructions as to what action was to be taken against the police...When 'An Seabhac' arrived back in Killarney from Tralee on Easter Sunday morning he went to the Volunteer Hall, met Michael Spillane and informed him that he had been speaking to Monteith in Tralee, and that he had delivered to Monteith orders from G.H.Q. Monteith said to 'An Seabhac' that he could not understand why headquarters put him in Kerry where he did not know an inch of the ground or a single man.

The arms and ammunition were at the bottom of the ocean, and what ammunition was on-hand would hardly suffice to give a round per head. Also on Easter Sunday morning, as previously arranged with Austin Stack, Michael J. O'Sullivan cycled to Tralee. His instructions from Michael Spillane were to remain in Tralee until 5 p.m. and then return to Killarney with final orders. In Tralee Michael J. O'Sullivan was asked by Paddy Cahill if he would be willing to take Monteith with him to Killarney, as it was a more mountainous district where he could be more easily hidden. O'Sullivan agreed but later in the day this was changed and it was decided that Monteith would march out to Ballymacelligott in the midst of the Ballymacelligott Company when the men were returning to their own area.

About 3.30 p.m. on Easter Sunday Pierce McCann Cashel, arrived in Killarney in his own car and gave McNeill's cancellation order to Michael Spillane verbally. McCann and Spillane were old friends; both had been at the Officers' Training Camp in Athlone in the previous September. Richard Fitzgerald, Lieutenant in Killarney Company, was at that Camp also. An enquiry by Spillane as to how he had received the cancellation order, McCann said that he had received it from The O'Rahilly who was on his way to Limerick to deliver a similar order there. McCann asked Spillane to send the order on to Tralee, and to make sure it arrived there before 5 p.m. Spillane sent James Galvin, a member of the Killarney Company and a native of Tralee, to Tralee with the order.

Michael Spillane then issued the cancellation order to the Companies under his command in the Killarney Battalion area, viz. Rathmore, Ballyhar, Listry and Killarney. This stopped all mobilisation in the area on Easter Sunday.

Michael J. O'Sullivan returned to Killarney from Tralee about 6.30 p.m. on Easter Sunday. He informed Michael Spillane of the different happenings in Tralee and told him that the cancellation order had been received while he was there. Spillane told O'Sullivan of McCann's visit during his absence, how McCann had got stranded without petrol, and that five gallons were supplied to him without a permit by John Thompson, Garage Owner, Killarney, 'An Seabhac' had remained in Killarney all day on Sunday, and on Monday he went to Caherciveen. Pat O'Shea and Jerry Sullivan went to Cork on Monday, but came back that night without any additional information.

On Easter Tuesday evening, about 7.30 p.m., Liam Scully, a native of Glenbeigh, arrived from Brigade Headquarters, Tralee, with orders to go out at midnight. Michael Spillane was preparing despatches in accordance with this order to send to Rathmore, Listry and Ballyhar when Scully returned and said not to send them out as further orders were coming. We do not know the explanation of this, but doubt if Scully could have got in touch with Tralee in the short time that elapsed between his first and second visit. Kathleen O'Sullivan had arrived in Killarney from Caherciveen looking for information or instructions. Michael Spillane had given her, for Diarmuid O'Connell, 'An Seabhac' – the order given by Scully, and she was about to leave when Scully returned and cancelled it. About an hour later Con Brosnan, a native of Tralee, brought a despatch from there. It was, 'Did Cork act, or will Cork act?' Paddy Cahill was anxious to get Cork, Kerry and Limerick out together. That despatch was carried by Jerry Company, Killarney, to Dan Dennehy, Captain of the Rathmore Company. Coffey was ordered not to leave Rathmore until the message was sent to Millstreet. Coffey reported back, saying that John Linehan, Rathmore, had carried the despatch and delivered it to Carmody and Twomey, Millstreet.

On Wednesday morning a despatch rider named Jack O'Leary from Tralee arrived to Michael Spillane enquiring of the whereabouts of Con Brosnan, and if Michael Spillane had got the despatch entrusted to Brosnan on the previous day. Spillane told O'Leary that he had ordered Brosnan to go to bed at Spicer's, Killarney, as he was completely worn out and was suffering from a disability to his eye. He informed O'Leary that Brosnan had delivered the despatch, that it had been sent on to Millstreet, but that no answer had been received from Cork. No reply was received from Cork to that despatch as far as we know. Considerable tension had developed in Kerry from Good Friday onwards. In Killarney all cars were commandeered by the police and no petrol could be sold without a permit from them. This was one result of Casement's landing at Banna, the disaster at Ballykissane Pier, Killorglin, where the car ran into the [River] Laune, and the breaking down of the second car on that mission two miles outside Killarney, near Laccabane. All this caused a state of unrest and made the police very active and alert. Michael Spillane spoke to Jimmie French on the street and asked him why his car had been commandeered. A policeman named O'Keeffe called French and asked him what Spillane was saying to him.

We had orders to evade arrest. This, with the unrest and uncertainty which prevailed, placed Killarney in what may be termed a state of siege and gave an air of war to the place. All were keyed up, and the police being on the qui vive created in Killarney a state that did not exist in hardly any other part of the country. The Officers were doing their best to keep everything up to pitch and have their men ready to go out, but all the orders, one cancelling another, caused undue worry and uncertainty. The shooting of two policemen by Jimmie Riordan at Pines on Easter Saturday added to the tension and to the alertness of the police. Every Volunteer was a marked man. To carry out orders, which were carried out, was extremely difficult, but, in spite of this, everything was ready and a state of preparedness existed to the last detail. All orders were carried out conscientiously.

Riobárd Langford,
Cork City.[24]

From about 1909 until the establishment of the Irish Volunteers, An Dún in Queen Street was the centre of all advanced national activity in Cork City... I was Secretary in 1912. The whole building was rented by the Gaelic League, but was sub-let at times or in part to various national or cultural bodies...

There was another Cork organisation which was active in Anti-British activities before the Volunteer movement started. It was the A.O.H. American Alliance. The following were members:- Tomás MacCurtain, Eamon Coughlan, Seán Good, Tadg Barry, Harry Lorton, Pat Harris, Jerry Fawsitt, Frank Healy, B.L., Cobh, Seán Ó Tuama, Seán O'Leary, Domhnal Óg O'Callaghan, Miceál Ó Cuill. From the O'Growney Branch of the A.O.H. American Alliance came all anti-British and anti-recruiting activity at that period. In the background there was always the I.R.B. under Seán O'Hegarty's control and its activities were exercised mainly through the members of these two organisations...All the Cork Volunteers went to Confession on Easter Saturday night. There was tension and everyone felt the day had come. There was no definite information about what was intended but the general that something more than an ordinary parade was due on Sunday. When the men assembled in the Hall on Easter Sunday morning MacCurtain distributed First

---

[24] B.M.H., W.S. 16.

Aid outfits – this was the first time they had been issued. Every available weapon was secured. Five rifles, which were held by the O'Sheas in Dominick Street, were not brought to Sheares Street men assembled. They were sent for and the parade did not move off until they arrived. One hundred and fifty-four Volunteers, officers and men, entrained at Capwell Station. Dr Jim Ryan arrived in the hall at Sheares Street with MacNeill's countermanding order after the parade had moved off to where he saw MacCurtain and MacSwiney. They had a car and went to Crooks town in it. The Volunteers left the train there and Sean O'Sullivan, who was in charge, was informed by MacCurtain that the exercises were cancelled.

We marched to Bealnablaith, met the Ballinhassig men there and the Ballinadee men at Kilmurray and all marched to Macroom. A meeting of Senior Officers was held at Macroom but I was not present. My impression is that MacCurtain and MacSwiney did not know on Sunday the arms ship was lost. There was much dissatisfaction when it became known that we were to return to Cork. Sean O'Sullivan, C. O'Gorman, P. Cotter and myself, amongst the officers, were in favour of staying in Macroom. We returned to Cork by train on Sunday evening and the men took their arms to their homes. There were no arms in the Hall except the arms of the Guard.

A Miss Perolz came from Dublin on a motor-bike on Monday with Pearse's message 'We start here at noon to-day.' She went to the Hall but there was no Senior Officer there. It was late on Monday evening when MacCurtain and MacSwiney arrived in Cork and saw this message for the first time. I did not see Miss Perolz but I heard she was in the Hall on Monday. Paddy Trahey was Guard Commander and was on duty at the Hall on Easter Monday. There was considerable confusion and everyone was worried by the absence of MacCurtain and MacSwiney. They stayed in the Hall on Monday night and the guard was maintained.

On Tuesday about 12 o'clock I was in the Hall and I saw the message. Its text was 'We start here at noon today.' It did not contain the words 'Carry out your instructions.' It was in manuscript on paper, about the size of an envelope. It was signed 'P.H.P.', not 'P.H. Pearse'. There was some question of the authenticity. Tomás said he had never known Pearse to sign in that way before. Mary

MacSwiney was in the Hall and she took part in the discussion about what to be taken. She said in effect: 'Was a fine body of men like the Irish Volunteers to be dragged at the tail of a rabble like the Citizen Army?' There was comment that the messenger was not a Volunteer but a Citizen Army messenger. I have the impression that a further message came in confirmation of Pearse's message but not see it nor the person who brought it. The messenger is supposed to have been a Miss Brennan, or someone who went under the name of Brennan, and a member of the Citizen Army. In any case, Tomás finally accepted the Pearse message as being genuine when it was known that fighting was actually taking place in Dublin.

I was in the Hall all day on Monday. The atmosphere was very tense and strained. The younger officers particularly wanted to fight, and were resentful of the waiting policy adopted by the leaders. They expressed their views, but the weight of the influence and authority of the older men – as they regarded the Brigade Officers – was against them. A lead from them would have taken the majority of the Cork men into the fight in some way. Action in the city may have been inadvisable, but there was nothing to prevent the Volunteers mobilising outside the city on Monday or Tuesday.

On Tuesday night a railwayman named Pat Duggan came to the Hall and said he had been called out to armoured train to Dublin. He was willing to train if he got instructions so. He saw Tomás and Terry but they would not take the responsibility of giving him an order. No move against the Volunteers was made by the Military or police up to the Thursday of Easter Week. On that day the Auxiliary Bishop, Dr Cohalan, was at a function at St. Francis Hall, Cove Street. He sent a message to MacCurtain and MacSwiney, and I, with, I think, Pat Trahey, was sent over to him. He would not discuss anything with us, but gave us a written message for the Brigade Officers. MacCurtain and MacSwiney saw him later and negotiations for the surrender of arms began. Lord Mayor Butterfield took part in these negotiations, and it was finally agreed to give the arms into the custody of the Lord Mayor at his house on the South Mall. The question of surrender was put to a vote of the men assembled in the Hall on the Monday after Easter Monday. The surrender had then taken place in Dublin. There were from 100 to 140 men in the Hall, and about 90 per cent of those present voted for the surrender, but all the arms were not, in fact, handed in to the Lord Mayor and I and others took the bolts out of the rifles that were handed in. The Volunteers did not believe the British would keep their side of the agreement, and were not surprised when they seized the rifles soon afterwards. The strongest opposition to the surrender came from the Junior officers.

List of Sources

Bureau of Military History Archive

B.M.H., W.S. 194

B.M.H., W.S. 920

B.M.H., W.S. 200

B.M.H., W.S. 694

B.M.H., W.S. 725

B.M.H., W.S. 264

B.M.H., W.S., 660

B.M.H., W.S. 826

B.M.H., W.S. 356

B.M.H., W.S. 251

B.M.H., W.S. 805

B.M.H., W.S. 318

B.M.H., W.S. 195

B.M.H., W.S. 386

B.M.H., W.S. 342

B.M.H., W.S. 887

B.M.H., W.S., 337

B.M.H., W.S. 489

B.M.H., W.S. 378

B.M.H., W.S. 347

B.M.H., W.S. 132

B.M.H., W.S. 16.

B.M.H., W.S. 348

B.M.H., W.S. 1,019

Publications

Clara Cullen (ed.), *The World Upturning: Elsie Henry's Irish Wartime Diaries, 1913–1919* (Dublin: Merrion Press, 2012). Extracts published courtesy of Dr Clara Cullen.

De Courcy Wheeler: Permission to reproduce courtesy of Alex Findlater and A. & A. Farmar Publishers.

Keith Jeffery (ed.), *The Sinn Féin Rebellion As They Saw It/Mary Louisa and Arthur Hamilton Norway* (Dublin: Irish Academic Press, 1999)

Keith Jeffery, *The GPO and the Easter Rising* (Dublin: Irish Academic Press, 2006)